MULTILINGUAL CONNECTORS

12 GAME-CHANGING PRINCIPLES OF BUILDING INTERCULTURAL CONNECTIONS WITHOUT LANGUAGE MASTERY

吴 笑 寒 WÚ XIÀOHÁN
DAISY WU

Copyright © Xiaohan Wu

First published in Australia in 2023
by KMD Books
Waikiki, WA 6169

All rights reserved. No part of this book may be used or reproduced by any means, graphic, electronic, or mechanical, including photocopying, recording, taping or by any information storage retrieval system without the written permission of the copyright owner except in the case of brief quotations embodied in critical articles and reviews.

Because of the dynamic nature of the Internet, any web addresses or links contained in this book may have changed since publication and may no longer be valid. The views expressed in this work are solely those of the author and do not necessarily reflect the views of the publisher and the publisher hereby disclaims any responsibility for them.

Typeset in Adobe Garamond Pro 12.5/18pt

 A catalogue record for this work is available from the National Library of Australia

National Library of Australia Catalogue-in-Publication data:

Multilingual Connectors/Daisy Wu

ISBN: 978-0-6455691-8-6
(Paperback)

This book is dedicated to:

My family in China who have heavily invested in me to pursue my dreams overseas.

Mr. Mingjie (Jason) Zhang, my high school English teacher in China, who helped me build a solid foundation and sustain my passion for learning my second language.

My mentors Ron Malhotra and Elinor Moshe, who have been instrumental in my success, my education and my Thought Leadership journey, without whom this book would not have come alive.

Prof. Robert H. Crawford, Prof. Priyan Mendis and A/Prof. Ajibade A. Aibinu from the University of Melbourne who've proven the concepts in this book and embody the amazing connections that shaped my trajectory in Australia as a Multilingual Connector.

And all the readers, who I hope to enable and inspire to live a better life on their own terms and to make quality connections.

CONTENTS

Foreword:
From Language Perfectionism To Intercultural Connection 1

Introduction 5

The Multilingual Connectors (MLC) Framework 14

Chapter 1:
Who Cares About The Language? 20

Chapter 2:
The Most Influential Person In Our Connections 34

Chapter 3:
The Language You Must Master To Master Anything... 55

Chapter 4:
Don't Work Harder On The Language 77

Chapter 5:
You Can Never Communicate In ONE Language..........101

Chapter 6:
'Non-Native English' Is Our Superpower 121

Chapter 7:
Decode The KPIs Of Your 'KPI's' 137

Chapter 8:
All Roads Lead To Rome 158

Chapter 9:
Make Time Your Friend 174

Chapter 10:
The LESS You Communicate, The MORE Mistakes You Make 197

Chapter 11:
Hurdles Are Not Barriers 217

Chapter 12:
It's Okay To Dislike Networking 240

About The Author 259

FOREWORD

FROM LANGUAGE PERFECTIONISM TO INTERCULTURAL CONNECTION

In Daisy Wu's *Multilingual Connectors,* we hear the voice of a courageous young woman from China telling the story of her realization that, to find a sense of belonging for a global audience, human connection matters far more than mastering perfect English.

As an educator, this truth—the core message of this book—is one that I hold to be fundamental. Language is a tool used to communicate: it is a means toward connection, not an end in itself. Today, scholars of social linguistics are increasingly critical of the concept of "correct" language use because they recognise that languages are living social practices, constantly evolving. They recognize that there is not just one version of English but many "Englishes", including multiple variants spoken in linguistically and culturally diverse communities worldwide. Indeed, as is pointed out early on in this book, on a global scale, speakers for whom English is not their first language vastly outnumber so-called "native speakers". In light of this "non-native" dominance, "correct" English seems more and more like a chimera. And it makes little sense to wear oneself out perfecting one's language to accord with this mythical gold standard if one consequently neglects the whole point of language learning: communication and social connection.

If all recent migrants and international students were able to grasp this realization early on as effectively as Daisy Wu has done, then their social, cultural, educational and personal journeys could be so much less burdensome and more rewarding. This book promises to help that happen.

Daisy Wu first arrived in Australia at age seventeen, to commence her studies in a bridging program geared toward undergraduate enrolment. I first met her in her hometown of Shanghai just prior to her departure. Over the intervening seven years, it has been truly remarkable to witness Daisy blossom from her old self—a very young, quiet teenager still closely looked after by her parents—into the confident, independent, high-achieving young professional whose voice we hear in this book.

At the time she travelled from Shanghai to Melbourne, like many other migrants from China, Daisy had absorbed a deep belief in the fundamental importance of mastering perfect English. During her first year in Melbourne, I saw her relentless, steely determination to develop and practice her mastery of new and obscure vocabulary, tricky local idioms, and intricate

MULTILINGUAL CONNECTORS

grammatical structures. It is unsurprising that Daisy assumed that such drills held the key to a sense of belonging in an English-dominant society—this idea is inculcated deeply in students by the way English is taught in China's mainstream education system.

It is to Daisy's credit that she has been able to shrug off this formalist approach to language learning and forge an alternative framework for mastering cross-cultural communication. As is outlined in depth in the pages of this book, this framework is based on honouring one's own unique cultural heritage, accent and perspective; letting go of the fear of failure; and trusting that the will to self-expression will lead to authentic personal connection across cultures, regardless of the formal (im)perfection of one's English.

Beyond these lessons about how best to approach cross-cultural communication, this book also holds many heartfelt and moving stories about its author's personal growth during her years in Australia, despite the very real social, cultural and academic challenges she has met along the way. The challenges faced by international students and migrants like Daisy are all too real: from historically entrenched Australian racism and xenophobia, to visa-based exclusion from professional opportunities, and deficits in institutional support for international students' and migrants' general welfare and wellbeing. Through all of this, Daisy Wu has survived and thrived. Her story makes for compelling reading, and the advice she imparts will be immensely valuable to future international students and migrants.

Integrating a wealth of research across self-help and corporate motivational literature, popular psychology and cross-cultural

DAISY WU

communication studies, this is a hugely important book. It holds the power to change dominant narratives not just on English learning but also, much more broadly, on the intercultural skills and opportunities of the new generation of migrants around the world today.

Fran Martin, Professor of Cultural Studies, The University of Melbourne, Melbourne, October 2023

INTRODUCTION

You may understand the rules of more than one language, but do you understand the rules of connecting with people? You may be able to translate between languages, but can you easily transform from your comfort zone to a new world of opportunities, one full of unknowns?

With globalisation gathering pace, the language learning market was valued at USD 40.2 Billion in 2021 worldwide, and estimated to reach USD 172.71 Billion by 2027. Clearly, language barriers remain at the forefront of many minds as one of the biggest perceived challenges in international communication. It is a popular belief that mastery of the official language(s) is one of the most direct roads to social integration in a brand new foreign society. A demonstration of this, an Australian National University poll in 2015 saw more than 90% of people who believed the ability to speak English was critical to 'being truly Australian' and that being born in the country was much less significant. Given such mainstream perceptions, language appears to be one of the most important enabling skills needed for sound and effective communication to survive and thrive in intercultural settings.

Did you know there are 2 billion non-native English speakers who weren't born into English-speaking households that dominate over 80% of the English-speaking world? Dominant as they are, these non-native speakers, including myself and probably you, are often identified as underrepresented populations in many social and professional contexts.

If English is not your first language, do you ever feel those who have managed to master the most common international language, like native British or American speakers, have better chances to achieve goals than you in the ever-expanding realm of opportunities?

Did you ever realise, that even with various intercultural communication challenges popularly associated with language barriers, you can convert your limitations into strengths, and disadvantages into advantages, if you are dedicated to understanding and mastering yourself before seeking to master any language?

What if I were to tell you, as an ordinary non-native speaker, you can still achieve extraordinary results in a foreign context without being highly proficient in a dominant language if you are highly skilled in connecting with people.

Yes, after months and years of hard work in classrooms and gaining real-life practice, you have probably advanced in a foreign language past the point of survival in order to graduate from your degree(s) and establish your career. Perhaps you already feel proud of how far you've come using your non-native language. Yet if you were to go beyond the functional interactions and everyday small talk to build stronger and deeper bonds,

MULTILINGUAL CONNECTORS

where would you see yourself on the spectrum of confidence and competence?

While you can command the language to work with your colleagues, go shopping and access professional services, do you always feel in your element in other personal and formal social interactions?

Can you express your feelings and thoughts easily within the limits of your words in most situations?

Do you still struggle to understand someone as an individual, despite the language barrier fading?

Do you often feel seen and heard in a conversation?

Do you feel limited by your language skills to pursue more people-oriented opportunities which better align with your personality or interests?

Is it challenging for you to find the time and space in the everyday busyness to maintain and advance relationships?

Do you see a wide gap between your self-confidence and language proficiency which holds you back from better opportunities and diversified networks?

Also, bear in mind that it's never just about the language; intercultural communications, as introduced before, can be a minefield with various well documented potential pitfalls in our international world.

There are a series of social forces driving these challenges, and in turn, the compulsion to advance language skills with the illusion that 'things will get better if my English is better'. In the same context, not everyone appreciates the differences between a contact and a connection, with the two concepts often getting mixed up on mainstream social media platforms. Even fewer people recognize that as foreigners, the more emphasis we place on language abilities in the bigger picture, the harder it is to convert a contact into a connection, and a connection into a comrade and/or confidant.

Who am I to make such a statement? After spending years improving my English to establish life in Australia as a Chinese immigrant, I became an award-winning young female achiever in male-dominated industries. I was selected to teach in a top-ranked university, speak at a TEDx event, interview on international podcasts and industry panels and feature on prominent media. Yet, you probably wouldn't believe that even though I was increasingly able to stay on top of translation to take on such amazing opportunities, I found communicating in a foreign language even more challenging than I had thought years before.

Growing up without a background of privilege and an English-speaking environment for seventeen years, I felt I must give at least 200% to everything to get the same results as a native English speaker in my university degrees and career. Over time in an immersive language environment, I could recognize and understand English that was spoken in multiple accents and at different paces, but I didn't adapt well to cultural and individual differences. I could read research papers, news articles and technical documents with greater ease, but didn't feel competent in reading people's minds. I could write professional emails and reports to perform routine tasks but would often scratch my head trying to frame short messages to prompt action and grow rapport with colleagues and acquaintances. I could speak more fluently and articulate my thoughts with decent grammar and advanced vocabulary but still didn't feel well understood and appreciated in certain situations. Looking around, some people even achieved what I wanted faster, without sophisticated English skills, in the same environment.

Ironically, as my English became better over time, I grew even more self-conscious, self-doubting, frustrated and confused when I kept struggling to navigate relationships and convert opportunities in a multicultural society. I felt like an imposter and too reserved to reveal this vulnerable side of me. When I mustered up the courage to discuss my problems with others of different linguistic backgrounds, most of them reacted in bafflement and downplayed the issue. 'Are you joking? Your English is so good and you've accomplished so much in only a few years. How could you (still) be struggling?' 'Take it easy! Don't be too hard on yourself!' 'Things will work out! You're still young…' 'Don't stress! I must have just landed that job with sheer luck! Your English is much better than mine so you will most definitely get a better position!'

Looking around, I felt even lonelier than when I first arrived in Australia to study with many Chinese-Asian peers, facing a lot of challenges but expectant about the journey ahead. Years have passed since then, and we've grown apart to the degree that we now are seemingly unable to relate to each other on the common ground of encountering a language barrier.

Indeed, connection was a missing element in many of my social ties. As an emotional state and intrinsic human need, it is 'the energy that exists between people when they feel seen, heard, and valued; when they can give and receive without judgement; and when they derive sustenance and strength from the relationship,' according to Dr. Brene Brown. As an essential skill and success determinator, it is 'the ability to identify with people and relate to them in a way that increases your influence with them,' in the words of John C. Maxwell. When language barriers occupied my mind for many years, 'connection' was only a foreign term. After I was more educated on its meanings in interpersonal contexts, I recognised how integral it is to thriving, not just surviving, in various aspects of life. Further to this, I realized I must work on something else rather than just the English language to improve interpersonal effectiveness.

While the 2021 Australian Census results imply that migrants' confidence and competence in English generally increases over time, such data, based on subjective self-assessment, should not be taken at face value. Various studies suggest the network with the local residents and migrants from other cultural and ethnic groups are vital contributors to a sense of true belonging. In practice, however, diversifying networks beyond one's own cultural and ethnic group is a common challenge for migrants. There is also mounting evidence that some migrants still face integration problems despite their advanced knowledge of the official language and education in the host countries to fill vital skills shortages. Evidently, despite the correlation between language mastery and adaptation to a foreign environment, language proficiency on its own is insufficient to bridge the gaps in social networking skills. Needless to mention, to break the socio-institutional barriers externally, an individual must first overcome a host of mental and cultural hurdles internal to themselves. For this reason, I felt obliged to write this book for you to provide an antidote to language mastery and a road map for mastering cross-cultural relationships without having to master foreign

MULTILINGUAL CONNECTORS

languages.

Because, from where I'm coming from, I see conventional education and societal customs as trapping millions of talented and promising non-native speakers like you and I in mental prisons and within the endless grind to learn the foreign language, instead of enabling us to thrive in cross-cultural settings. Considering the additional social challenges in a foreign context, we are extremely vulnerable to getting caught up in the translation, while overlooking the other essential elements for connecting to who we're communicating with.

As an ordinary non-native English speaker who's achieved extraordinary results without perfection or native proficiency in English, I wrote this book to disrupt the common perception about language abilities as an overrated hurdle and demystify the key to building genuine connections instead of superficial contacts across cultures. I have packaged my shared experience in a multicultural network that was once or is currently confronted with language barriers, together with the powerful mental models and life philosophy I have learnt from my inspiring connections, without whom I couldn't have accomplished what I have.

Though language learning, communication and personal development are widely studied, at the intersection of these multi-billion dollar industries, there is scant literature which provides a structured and actionable framework to tackle the multi-faceted challenges of building cross-cultural connections. Even with the non-language related hurdles broadly recognized and studied, mainstream education and training on intercultural communication still display a dominant focus on language acquisition. Meanwhile, there is a corresponding gap in general self-help resources, many not tailored to the psychographics of foreign language learners to set them up for success outside of the classroom and textbooks.

I've discovered the missing pieces of the puzzle, which I will share with you through 12 game-changing principles vital to building the skill set necessary to achieve connections outside of your own culture. These are captured in the 'Multilingual Connectors (MLC) Framework' I constructed to encapsulate the philosophy for the book.

I totally relate to how challenging and exhausting it can be to navigate the extra mental load of communicating in a non-native language. I know how frustrating it is when you have spent so much time and energy to upgrade your language skills and qualifications, yet are still not able to improve the status quo as soon as you wish. That said, I've also deciphered how easy it is to bypass the language hurdle to achieve 200% more results with 50% less effort towards the language and potentially other technical skills.

I can't wait to share my secret sauce with you that I wish I'd had much earlier on. I want you to stop feeling unconfident, undervalued and unfulfilled because of your language abilities. I want you to know how to work smarter, not harder, on the foreign language so there is even more time and space for you to find and build your tribe with like-minded connections. I want to inspire and enable you to break barriers and unlock opportunities regardless of how proficient you are in a foreign language.

What are you waiting for? To learn the secrets to fast-track your dreams with no language barriers, read on!

MULTILINGUAL CONNECTORS

Disclaimer:

The experiences, viewpoints and writings in this book are my own, except where a quotation or reference to a third party is made.

The name, position and institution of all individuals identified in the book is correct at the time of publishing.

THE MULTILINGUAL CONNECTORS (MLC) FRAMEWORK

Connecting with other people requires a broad repertoire of skills and mindset in addition to language abilities. With the multi-faceted challenges of cross-cultural and intercultural connections popularly associated with language barriers, there is hardly any practical frameworks available which capture the skills and mindsets instrumental to overcoming these challenges. To fill this gap, I've created the 'Multilingual Connectors (MLC) Framework' to encapsulate the how-to on implementing the central idea of the book, which is also at the heart of my Thought Leadership. Through the mastery of powerful mental models and essential non-technical skills, one can be effective in building connections across cultures without advanced or native-like proficiency in a foreign language.

As illustrated below, the MLC Framework consists of 3 foundational building blocks: a basic to intermediate command of a foreign language, mastery of communication essentials and understanding of human psychology and behaviours:

The MLC Framework

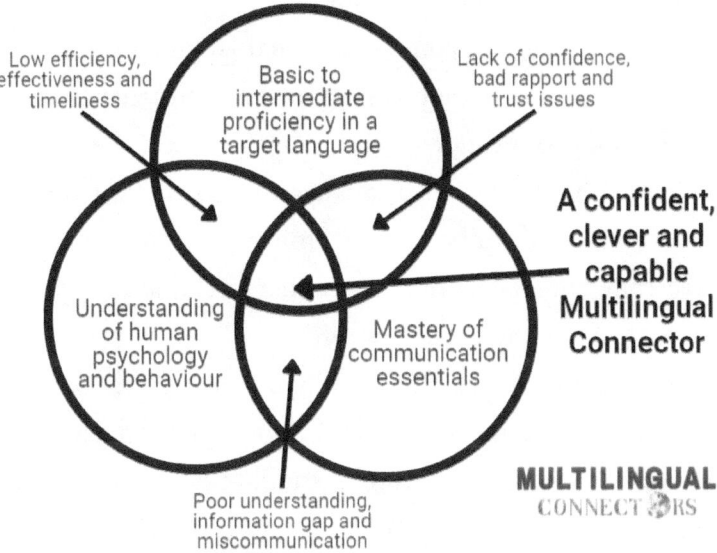

Building Block 1: Basic to intermediate proficiency in a target language

The first element relates to your proficiency in the target language. I deliberately word the criteria in broad terms which are subject to interpretation, instead of referencing specific matrices in mainstream language proficiency tests. Appreciating language as an intercultural communication tool, one does need a basic foundation of vocabulary and grammar in order for literal comprehension to be easier. You should strive towards the level where you can get your point across by using the simplest words possible. Ideally, you'll advance beyond the task-oriented functional language for your job and daily routines in a foreign community (e.g., shopping, travelling) to a level where you can easily understand and express your feelings and thoughts in that language. Just imagine yourself to be somewhere above the bottom line, wherever you define it in your circumstances, but not significantly advanced or sophisticated.

If you are relatively confident in that language but still have to pick up the book to help you solve the riddles that come with trying to build connections, you can bypass this evaluation while keeping the habit of continuous learning. If any of these still sound vague or arbitrary, just remember it is neither native-like competency nor anywhere closer to that level that I vouch for or encourage you to endeavour towards.

I often come across this term 'native like' in the narratives around language acquisition. While language proficiency holds its own place in the big picture, it should not be worshipped as the most critical hurdle to human connections. Particularly, the excessive focus on advancing language abilities in ignorance of the other critical skill sets needs to be addressed, which the other two MLC building blocks encompass.

Building Block 2: Mastery of communication essentials

The second building block is your command of communication essentials. Generally, there are three categories of communication: verbal (oral) communication, written communication and non-verbal communication, all of which will be discussed in this book through the lens of a non-native speaker.

To build a constellation of productive social networks, this pillar also extends into meeting and connecting with certain people at the right place and time as being most conducive to forging and accelerating connections. It requires you to strategically plan and manage your dedications to your existing and prospective connections in the interest of your time and resources as well as that of other people.

Benjamin Franklin famously said, 'If you fail to plan, you are planning to fail!' Not everything happens by chance or luck. Given how critical quality connections are to your professional success and social well-being, you must adopt this goal as a lifelong project and recognise its imperativeness as a skill. It is only through meticulous planning and execution that you can maximise the chance of turning a stranger to a contact and a contact to a connection, a connection to an advocate or confidant and so forth. These all fall under the non-language related factors for communication with the objective of connecting, which this book will uncover.

Building Block 3: Understanding of human psychology and behaviour

Lastly, to communicate effectively and steer relationships to a deeper and more meaningful level, you must understand the behaviours and psychological constructs of other people, as well as that of your own. This does not necessarily mean you need to become a psychology expert or have formal education in this arena, though it would be helpful.

In principle, the process of interacting with people always requires energy. What generates the energy? Movements. In this context, movements encompass not only our interactions with the outside world but also what is going on within our inner world. If we liken ourselves to engineers, we need to understand the fundamental rules and basic principles in order to design and engineer the solutions to the complex problems in our relationships. Though human beings can understand and use logic, statistics show that 90% of human decisions are made based on emotions. According to Amity Hope in The Rules of Persuasion, in most persuasive situations, people react upon emotions and perceptions and then use logic and fact to justify their emotionally driven actions. This further underscores the criticality of understanding the mechanics of emotions which can ignite, fuel or burn connections.

First things first, before working on your relationships with others, you should start with inner work both on and for yourself. Your connections come through you and should serve you well. It all starts with you. Using the project management analogy above, you are the one responsible for these bonds and ties from conception, design, construction and maintenance (plus disposal, if applicable to any). Not only do you need to be clear about who you are, what you value and stand for, and what you want to achieve in your life, you also need to be highly cognisant of your skills and mindsets, which are critical to interpersonal success. Regarding the mindset, it refers to a series of self-perceptions and beliefs you hold that shape your behaviours, outlooks and mental attitudes. 'It is your attitude, more than your aptitude, that will determine your altitude.' I've always liked and often refer to this famous quote of Zig Ziglar in support of the notion that mindset always comes before skill set in determining a person's life results.

Understanding and managing yourself behaviourally and mentally is key to self-mastery, which gives you control over the one variant you can control in any situation: yourself.

MULTILINGUAL CONNECTORS

Self-mastery over your own thoughts, emotions, words and actions can totally transform yourself as well as the results in any arena of your life, be it mastering a foreign language or achieving intercultural competence. It lays a foundation for the understanding and command of other people's emotions, beliefs, values and goals with the aim of fostering the bond. Excellent emotional mastery of both oneself and other people is a defining character of Multilingual Connectors. In essence, our emotion is the experience of energy moving through the body which, as mentioned, has the power to make or break a connection.

Applied properly, the MLC framework will also enable you to exploit and maximise your unique advantages as non-native speakers, which this book will unveil. Perspective is everything. Do you see yourself as disadvantaged and hindered because you are foreign to the dominant language and culture in your surroundings? Have you ever realised how blessed you are to know more than one language – which is more than many people? Does it fascinate you the idea that you can leverage exactly what differentiates you from the native-speaking and monolingual counterparts to achieve the same if not better results in leveraging a multicultural network to fulfil your dreams?

Just like languages, connection skills are also learnable to build up interpersonal and intercultural competence. Wouldn't you rather become a confident, clever and capable Multilingual Connector to bypass the hurdle of language and defy the mainstream narratives with exceeding social effectiveness? This is explored more in the rest of the book.

CHAPTER 1

WHO CARES ABOUT THE LANGUAGE?

"People don't care how much you know until they know how much you care." — *Theodore Roosevelt*

Growing up in China, I believed my English must be very good in order to have a bright future. Not only has the language become the *lingua franca* of business, politics, education and tourism in our international world, the ability to use English has also been considered a significant identifier when it comes to standing out in a competitive university environment in my home country. In school, exam pressures made us embrace an unforgiving attitude toward errors in grammar, spelling, punctuation and word choice. The definition of good and bad English was pretty much based on how much we resembled the native speakers with accuracy being an unrelenting benchmark.

It is in such conditions that I was first exposed to the radical

MULTILINGUAL CONNECTORS

idea of not caring too much about English as a second language during high school:

'Just a thought Mr. Zhang ... If I said the sentence that way to a native speaker (where "the" was incorrectly omitted before a noun and added before the other), the other person should be able to understand me regardless, right?' wondered my classmate – we'll call him Alex.

'Hmmm ... probably ...' said Mr. Zhang, our English teacher.

'Then why are we working so hard to learn the grammar if we could still communicate with foreigners without getting the words 100% correct. Who cares!' politely, Alex kept following his curiosity.

'In some cases, the other person might still get what you've said when there are mistakes in your grammar. However, it doesn't make your English sound authentic and without mastering advanced grammar and phrases, you won't be able to outperform (other non-native speakers) and impress the native speakers,' replied Mr. Zhang, smiling.

When writing this book nearly a decade since then, I still vividly remember the tone, facial expression and body language of Alex when he was saying 'Who cares!' It made me chuckle in the first instance and, back then, with the prospect of studying in Australia, I really wished I could embrace such a carefree attitude about improving my English and prove him right after staying abroad for a while, however unrealistic it seemed.

After I embarked on the journey to live in Australia, there were multiple points when I would recall this moment and feel like exclaiming to Mr.Zhang and Alex if they were by my side: 'Who cares!' And I would finish the sentence with a bitter expression: 'Nobody cares … even when my English is much better now.'

LIFE DIDN'T BECOME BETTER EVEN WHEN MY ENGLISH WAS BETTER

In my high school days, without a shadow of doubt, I almost unconditionally accepted my teacher's words. When I bid farewell to my colleagues a year later to study in Australia, I was grateful to Mr. Zhang for giving me a foundation of grammar and vocabulary even though in a traditional curriculum, we did not spend much time practising speaking. I was determined to improve my English to become more native-like and achieve my goals overseas to make him proud.

When I first arrived, Melbourne was already a popular destination for Chinese-Asian migrants, so people could easily guess my nationality just from my look and dressing style even before I started talking. In the bridging course I started in, I studied with Asian colleagues and after class, most of us spent a lot of time with those speaking our mother tongues. I also lived with a Chinese host family in Melbourne's largest Chinese community. To some degree my limited social circle back then strengthened my fear over the stigma of speaking 'broken English' and being recognized as someone from an ethnic group where people stereotypically are not good at speaking the English language.

Under a 'go hard or go home' mentality, from day one of arriving in Melbourne, I pushed hard to fix my thick Chinese accent and expand my writing and conversational skills. When I struggled to find someone to practise English with, I would talk

MULTILINGUAL CONNECTORS

to myself in my bedroom and in the shower – which scared my host family. When commuting, I would listen to TED Talks to hone my listening proficiency and check in on a phone app to learn vocabulary everyday. When travelling and queuing, I would sometimes also mock conversations with an imaginary person on the other side of the phone. Besides, I frequently wrote English social media posts to improve my feel for the language and reinforce the memory of the new words and expressions.

Down the track, my efforts paid off and many people gave me a beam of hope: 'You've only lived here for a few years but you speak English so well!' 'You are a wordsmith!' 'I almost couldn't tell you grew up in a mandarin-speaking country ...' I was admitted to my dream university with a scholarship and luckily got my first industry job in the second year. I could see myself making good progress in outgrowing the language barrier and felt I deserved more and better in my dream land: a decent job in a renowned company, strong relationships and friendship with people from various parts of the world, a supportive social network, a home away from home, and being able to public speak in English – all which I grew up secretly dreaming about. As my English skills and professional experience gradually built up, I felt a bit more confident about attending networking events, taking on leadership roles at volunteering ventures and applying to top-ranked companies.

Just when the stars seemed to be aligning, a series of new challenges came my way.

With advanced English and local industry experience my university classmates were jealous of, I felt entitled to better job opportunities. Despite this, reality slammed me in the face in the hunt for my second job. On several occasions, the person hired for my desired position, was someone whose English wasn't as good as mine, and was someone who had seemingly less relevant qualifications and experience for that particular role. I actually went through way more trials and tribulations to land my second job than I did for my first job, contrary to the common notion that 'the first step is always the hardest'.

While I demonstrated solid technical skills to be promoted twice within six months in a leading multinational firm, I was advised to improve verbal confidence in the performance review. On the job, I had no difficulties in finishing tasks in front of a computer most of the time, but fear and nervousness still haunted me as I tended to over-prepare for English communications, especially for presentations and meetings with key stakeholders. I cannot understate the extra mental load that comes with trying to think on my feet in a fast-paced environment while trying to translate a foreign language at the same time, such as how difficult it is to stay sane in confrontational situations.

Transitioning in a culturally diverse big corporation, I was initially at a loss for how to bond with colleagues at all levels, instead of only superficially knowing each other as a name in the organisation chart and email chains. Coupled with introversion, I worried not being sociable and consistently confident in speaking English in all settings would cost me opportunities in both internal and external contexts. I didn't want to just keep my head down and get things done day in and out like a cog in the machine. To have a career, not simply a job, I wished to develop more quality relationships with like-minded people from different cultures who could be my comrades, mentors and partners

MULTILINGUAL CONNECTORS

on the job and beyond.

As a leader at volunteering ventures, I felt frustrated when my team members did not perform to expectations and I struggled to fathom and work around certain behavioural and personality differences. Although we eventually managed to perform the tasks and deliver amazing projects, the team dynamics were not up to par and my self-esteem took a hit. There were countless times where I simply couldn't move the needle with well-worded messages which I believed should get the point across with minimal translation issues.

Fresh in my tutoring role, I spent a lot of time preparing for university teaching, rehearsing what I would say nearly word by word, despite knowing the subject content inside and out as I was one of the top-performing graduates in my cohort. After being proudly made one of the youngest tutors in the faculty, I was still reeling from imposter syndrome and felt very insecure about being judged by those students who spoke much better English than me. Despite my good intentions of sharing my industry experience and university journey with my students who were freshers, I was only being met with confusing or absent looks on many faces. At one point the only solution I believed would work was to strictly adhere to the teaching plan, even when I could have expanded on some topics from my own experience for the students' benefit. Somehow though, even when I did deliver everything as per the syllabus, when the class was drawing to a close, it was clear that the students weren't taking in the information, and some students' impatient body language began to bruise my ego.

Some people may have admired and recognized my

achievements, but they never seemed keen to befriend me, clearly unaware that was something I wanted. Equally, I respected many of my connections for what they had accomplished, yet could hardly imagine developing a closer connection with them personally. I was able to stay on top of small talk and task-oriented communications but often felt drained and empty. Besides the main business, I tended to hold lots of reservations about stepping out and giving anything a chance, even when my English was enough to initiate basic general conversation.

I pretty much grew to a stage where my translation skills were much more developed and less problematic for me than years prior. Even so, in the day-to-day there were occasions where I wasn't sure what exactly to say and how to navigate my relationships with other English-speaking people. In and outside of the nine-to-five, I found myself in tricky situations every so often where I would still feel at my wit's end to deal with interpersonal challenges in a foreign setting – even with the language barrier factored out of the equation. Meanwhile, I had an increasingly intense feeling that I'd simply increased my contact list, but had made few genuine connections in a foreign country, even though I was seen as a well-connected young achiever in many people's eyes.

Such sentiments were exacerbated during the COVID-19 pandemic when loneliness hit me hard in one of the world's longest lockdowns, during which I had minimal social support to navigate various personal challenges.

'Who cares!' In that unprecedentedly trying period, such a critical voice often echoed in my headspace when I either received or imagined rejection after reaching out to some of my close contacts for emotional support. Such experiences were indeed humbling and shattered the illusion I once held that things would work out eventually only if I continued advancing my English skills.

THE MISSING PIECES

What was going wrong in those moments when I kept struggling interpersonally in an English speaking environment, despite my improved language proficiency? Somewhere down the personal development journey, I found some clues in the core concept of John C. Maxwell's book *Everyone Communicates, Few Connect*. The central focus of the book blew my mind – the idea that many people seek connection through communication, but fail to recognize that connection is much more than the relaying of information. It was overwhelming, humbling yet relieving to come into the realisation with the help of literature as such, that for as long as I was fixated on mastering authentic English as a non-native, I was predominantly focused on communicating to people in the right words but not so much connecting with them in the right ways, which remained a foreign concept for me for a long time.

It also struck me that while I had mastered the use of the past, present and future tenses and punctuation in grammar, I felt challenged to find time and space to advance relationships in everyday busyness. Besides understanding the order of words and how sentence structure worked, I still would fall short of reading between the lines. Many times I may have beautifully said what I wanted to say but not necessarily what the other person needed or wanted to hear. Even though I could skilfully apply connectors like 'and', 'or' and 'but' to connect phrases, words, or clauses to one another, I didn't have the formula for the bonding ingredients to connect myself with others.

The distinction between communicating and connecting, however nuanced it first appears, should not be too hard to grasp with reference to our own experiences. Whether in your native or foreign language, you should already know someone who speaks eloquently but hardly keeps you interested, convinced or motivated to take action in favour of the other person. There might also be someone you know who is far from being sophisticated and articulate in a dominant language but has a commanding presence that draws people in and makes others feel well supported, comfortable, and understood in their company.

From that standpoint, I was more able to put into perspective why I wasn't becoming significantly more interpersonally effective while outgrowing the language barrier. In fact, it should've dawned on me that where English proficiency is taken for granted, there are still people who do not achieve desired results with high interpersonal skills despite being born into the dominant language. As a demonstration of this, there is mounting evidence that in international business, native English speakers are failing to integrate and gain ground due to their shortfalls in tailoring their English in the intercultural context.

It follows that languages are better viewed as a medium for communication across borders, or a means to an end, with the end being meaningful connections fostered with other people vital to our well-being and development. Furthermore, it goes without saying that becoming more eloquent and well-spoken may afford you more respect and attention as you become

MULTILINGUAL CONNECTORS

someone to listen to rather than someone who's opinion is disregarded under the influence of social and linguistic bias. On its own merits though, language proficiency is at best one dimension of a person's competencies. Although such functional competencies may assist you in commanding due regard, they do not automatically make it easier to increase your likeability and build rapport with others.

As a subjective and vague concept, your likeability can generally be reflected in your ability to invoke positive sentiments and attitudes in others. Within the literature, Tim Sanders introduces four elements of likeability in his book *The Likeability Factor*: friendliness, relevance, empathy and realness.

Friendliness requires you to exude a positive attitude towards others and communicate in a welcome fashion.

Relevance depends on to what extent you and the other person connect and relate to each other's wants, needs and life interests.

Empathy manifests in your ability to put yourself in other's shoes and see things from their vantage point.

The last element, realness, is often used interchangeably with authenticity, simply meaning being truthful and genuine.

You should notice from the above definitions that there is barely any reference to language mastery or other functional skills as key determinants of likeability. Intuitively, it might feel easier to demonstrate these defining qualities in your native language as you can express yourself more to the point with greater ease. However, it is fundamentally not your words and accent, but rather your personal traits and characteristics that mainly contribute towards your likeability and ground for connecting, which do not largely rely on words to convey and are nearly impossible to fake. Recognizing this, you should not discount your ability to connect with others who do not speak your first language based on self-evaluated language ability.

THE LANGUAGE IS NEVER THE BIGGEST BARRIER

Truly, the difficulties of learning and applying a foreign language cannot be downplayed for many, needless to mention not everyone has the same starting point. While I still got caught up in the translation every so often, I could feel various other mental loads weighing me down and pulling me back. I hadn't quite noticed these mental loads in the beginning, when I'd been more preoccupied with overcoming the language barrier. Somewhere beyond the limit of my language, there appeared to be a series of other hurdles I couldn't identify let alone overcome. In reflection of my own experience, here are some of my biggest lessons in this context:

First and foremost, connecting is largely about other people rather than ourselves. People naturally focus more on their own interests than those of who they are interacting with. You should have come across this widely touted notion that nobody cares how much you know until they know how much you care (about them, as a common interpretation). When using a foreign language, it is normal to be self-conscious and concerned about how you will make the other person feel and think. Yet if you are to be brutally honest, who do you actually pay more attention to in such settings most of the time, the other person or yourself?

Further to the above, connection is a function of value. In

MULTILINGUAL CONNECTORS

my understanding, others will not unconditionally connect to what you know and have achieved until you demonstrate you can apply your skills and resources to provide value for them. Provided the rule of scarcity, wherever proficiency in a target language is a given, you can by no means solely count on language skills to stand out and be considered as a valuable person. Moreover, don't forget that an individual's value can not only be professional or functional, but also emotional and relational – whereby others experience positive feelings with you in the company or spirit. With a vast body of research underscoring the importance of emotional and social intelligence, the mastery of human psychology and behaviour is universally paramount and cannot be easily compensated with technical competencies in any area.

In this light, language can facilitate functional connections but not necessarily emotional connections. Essentially, through a common language, people are seeking to understand each other as an individual in anticipation of further bonding, who cannot be holistically defined or evaluated by the skills in any language. Over the years of living in a multicultural city, I've crossed paths with inspiring individuals from diverse backgrounds, who, even with average or below average English levels, still managed to defy odds and break barriers to establish themselves on a foreign land. While I remember feeling wishful and mind-blown by some of the non-native speakers who speak beautiful English without growing up in the language, their language proficiency may only have captured my attention and curiosity in the moment. Further on, however, it is those who displayed positive qualities and other idiosyncrasies on relatable grounds which moved me on a personal and emotional level that I gravitated towards and cultivated social bonds with.

Reflecting on my journey, language barriers faded over time but it certainly did not bridge the cracks in my confidence, self concept and beliefs. It hit me that language barriers are under the guise of self-constructed mental barriers at the root cause of many setbacks. Therefore, in the interpersonal context, language difficulties must not be dealt with in isolation. It also follows that self mastery must come before language mastery to master human connections across cultures.

THE REASON TO CARE

So, who cares about the language? I surely do and believe we all should.

Undeniably, to a certain degree, foreign language acquisition does require our due regard to increase the access to a broader realm of opportunities in the increasingly globalised world. That said, after all, whichever language we communicate in, it is human beings that we are interacting with who are both logical and emotional creatures. In this perspective, language proficiency cannot stand on its own outside the other enabling qualities you need to connect with people from different parts of the world.

It may seem like some people are gifted with an attractive personality and strong communication skills that draws others in. As non-native speakers, it is totally natural for you to imagine that those with native or native-like proficiency in a dominant language have many advantages over you to establish life in a foreign country. The fact is however, anyone can learn to communicate in ways that enable them to consistently build strong

MULTILINGUAL CONNECTORS

connections, as bestselling author and leadership expert John C. Maxwell identified.

Besides, there is something even better for you to know and explore in the next chapter to set the tone for the whole book – that each of you already knows someone who can ensure you acquire these practical skills to master connection without mastering languages. Keep reading!

CHAPTER 2

THE MOST INFLUENTIAL PERSON IN OUR CONNECTIONS

"God helps those who help themselves."

'Connecting is all about others.' This notion partially holds true in that every relationship is a two-way street and we should place emphasis on other people who can significantly impact our trajectory and results. Yet a literal interpretation of such a notion from John C. Maxwell's book has the danger of ignoring the most influential person in your network, the person reading this chapter right now – yourself!

I have learned from my mentors, without whom this book could not have been created, that we can and should take full ownership of our life results. My own take is that other people may be willing to support you in the ways they believe helpful to you, but only you know what really works best for you. It also does not serve you right if you bend yourself to what others want all the time in nearly all relationships. In every decision you make on the journey of building connections, there must be at least some vested interest that relates to your visions and goals.

It is in this spirit that I hope you can start reconsidering your role and the influence you have in your relationships, be it personal or professional, and feel more convicted and empowered in doing this. Though people rarely succeed alone and from time to time need to rely on other people as key stakeholders in your success and progress, you should not take the back seat when it comes to determining where you want to go, how you'll reach your goals and who you'll bring along the journey.

DEFINE THE MEANING OF SUCCESSFUL RELATIONSHIPS ON YOUR OWN TERMS

The fundamental question

Before even embarking on figuring out how to build meaningful relationships in your non-native language, you first have to be clear about the critical relationship with yourself: What is important to you? What does meaningful even mean to you? What do you need to accomplish or experience to be able to honestly tell yourself you are doing well in making connections abroad?

I once believed it was all too important to make friends with native speakers so that my English would become very good and I could thereby live a good life in Australia. After years of adhering to this mentality, I realised how confining and ineffective this belief was in a multicultural society and had yet to discover the full context of my ambitions and dreams in this country. For one thing, as I already shed light on in the opening chapter, communicating smoothly in any language with someone does not guarantee you will connect closely and grow meaningful relationships from there. Moreover, language is not the end goal. I gradually recognized that what I wished to achieve with bettering my English skills was to gain access to someone who I could lean on as a confidant, someone who I could share similar interests with and to pursue goals together as comrades, who I could look up to and learn from as a mentor, and anyone who could open my eyes to new perspectives and possibilities that they bring along with their unique being.

Down the path, I built a myriad of connections from various cultures and many of these relationships fulfilled more than one of the aforementioned objectives. This is far from what I initially imagined based on what I saw on the social media posts of my peers living overseas before starting my own journey: house parties, social drinks, sports games, coffee catch-ups, road trips, office functions, often with a few western faces in the photos. Later, I got to experience social interactions as such but not all of them turned out to be effective means to meet and connect with most of the key contacts I have now. Besides, I had shifted my obsession with connecting with native English speakers to instead find my circles in a culturally diverse society. Since everyone has their own definition of meaningfulness, these types of social ties may hold a greater space in others' minds but no longer my own, and surely, you should make your own decisions.

I would encourage you to reflect regularly and record your responses to these key questions:

- Based on your own definition, what are the top three most meaningful relationships you have had in your life? What made them so?
- What do you feel in those relationships?
- Why are you motivated to keep in touch with certain individuals?
- What makes you gravitate to each other?

Your answers here are critical as they will guide you towards building a constellation of connections to fulfil your goals.

Fitting in vs belonging

Another common issue confronting many immigrants is that they still feel outcast and as though they are outsiders after years of living in their host country. In both real life and on social media, the compulsion of immigrants to integrate in their local community can be widely observed. While there are a range of factors causing the feeling of marginalisation, it is worth examining the expectation of social integration in a foreign country which generates the pressure and exacerbates the feeling of isolation and underachievement within non-native speakers.

Consistent with my early impressions, blending in with native speakers or who we identify as 'locals' is commonly viewed as a strong signal of social success overseas. Even though the quality of your network cannot be evaluated superficially, in the minds of many international students and immigrants, both current and prospective, these images of assimilation they often see on social media about overseas life, go on to form the reference points as benchmarks of their own performance. While many immigrants who grew up in their country of origin believe they cannot fully outgrow their cultural legacy and embrace everything in their host culture, many still wish for a diversified network outside of their cultural origins where they feel they belong.

The pressure to fit in is so pronounced for immigrants worldwide. Often, I see people like us displaying a tendency to seek approval and acceptance in a foreign environment but still struggle with a low sense of belonging regardless of external achievements. In her book *Atlas of the Hearts*, Brene Brown explains the differences between fitting in and belonging. Fitting in is being accepted for being like everybody else and other people do not really care if you become a part of their group, though it is where you strive to be. In contrast, belonging requires the people you surround yourself with to accept you for who you are – not the false personas you create to be more similar to them – they want you to be a member of their social circle as the true you.

The language barrier I personally struggled with faded as time passed but it did not help me much in closing the gap between myself and those from other cultures, some of whom inherited distinctive appearances from their own cultural heritage including that of my own but thought and behaved differently. I am constantly reminded of where I came from when I feel lost whenever people talk about AFL (Australian Football League, a company which operates the competition of Australian rules football) and gulp down beers one jug after another in a crowded pub after work where the background conversations and music make it even harder to catch the conversations. When I first started out attending networking functions, I would also regret

MULTILINGUAL CONNECTORS

not having a hearty Asian meal before the nighttime event catered with a spread of olives, cheese and cold meat paired with alcohol. Initially, I was extremely worried about these as predictors of my ability to integrate into the 'Aussie' life, though it was based on limiting beliefs around fitting in, which was mixed up with the feeling of belonging that I ultimately desire.

I eventually found my tribe in a multicultural community. Simply, I did something quite counterintuitive, which was reinforcing some of my own lifestyle and traditions. I would openly talk about my habits and likings, such as food preferences and everything else that made life in Melbourne different from my hometown, Shanghai – to either bridge or divert conversations. By dedicating a lot of time after work to volunteering and piano learning instead of partying and playing sports, it's inevitable that I couldn't keep the conversation long with certain people, including some of my colleagues. Even so, as I kept up with these activities, I broadened my social circle with other people whose company I truly found enjoyable and inspiring. As these engagements were increasingly visible to my existing network on social media, they also became topical in some of our interactions where I was invited to share my latest experience. Leveraging their curiosity, I also earnt the opportunity to lead conversation from there till other points of connection emerged.

> *"True belonging doesn't require us to change who we are; it requires us to be who we are."* — Brene Brown

Back then, I already saw myself practising the two key hurdles to belonging identified by Brene Brown: vulnerability and self-acceptance. Counterintuitively, as Brene identifies, you will feel you truly belong somewhere when you sense more freedom to express your individuality without worrying it will negatively affect your belonging. You do not have to and should not give up any part of yourself in order to belong. Within hundreds and thousands of non-native speakers and immigrants, there exists a large subculture of people including myself who are just like you, those who know the delicate balance between cherishing your roots and staying true to yourself. Those who have dealt with constant questions about their appearances, languages, living habits and traditions which may not be akin to others in their environment. If you identify as one of these people, you already belong.

YOUR CONNECTIONS ARE ONLY AS GOOD AS YOU

See yourself the way you want others to see you

In its most basic definition, self-image refers to how you see yourself. It is the collective of all the beliefs and concepts you have about yourself in all aspects, physical, mental, intellectual, financial, interpersonal, etc. Self-image plays a crucial role in building successful relationships in your non-native language because it directly impacts your self-esteem and confidence. Besides, how you see yourself relates closely to how you believe others see you. Do you evaluate yourself largely based on what others think of you? Did you know that other people actually evaluate you based on how you view yourself? In fact, other people respond to you positively or negatively according to the way you present yourself,

MULTILINGUAL CONNECTORS

which is always consistent with your self-image. Naturally we tailor our messages and conduct to different people based on how we define them in our eyes, on the basis of what we know about them from what they present to us. Intuitively, are you more or less inclined to judge or question someone who comes off confident and prepared, compared to the other people who have even better knowledge and experience but appear not self-assured and unprepared? Fundamentally, the world sees you the way you see yourself and other people end up accepting you on your own evaluation of yourself.

> *"To change your behaviour for good, you need to start believing new things about yourself."* — James Clear, Author of Atomic Habits

As rudimentary as it might sound, you must stop believing who you are not, which prevents you from living out who you can and should be! You can still feel socially incompetent and stop short of showing up confidently, even after consuming lots of self-help resources to improve your social skills in another language or culture. You could have excellent communication skills, rich industry experience and solid track records to lead conversations and impart what you know, but cannot see yourself as a valuable source of knowledge so your behaviours will perpetuate this belief and keep you where you are. As a consequence of this, you are passed over for leadership and mentoring opportunities and people hardly approach you during networking, merely because you never appear keen and competent to exchange your knowledge and thoughts, instead of other people overlooking you due to bias and discrimination which you might speculate as the main reason in all cases. Identity reframing is thus highly relevant to surviving and thriving in a foreign environment, as the following chapter will illuminate. It can help unlock your potential and move you away from a diminished and crippling self-image, to counteract marginalisation and make yourself truly belong.

Take them off the pedestal

Do you sometimes feel you are less than someone who commands your non-native language fluently? Do you feel extremely humble and nervous in front of those with greater social status and achievements? Have you met anybody who falls into these categories and behaves in a way that arouses your self-consciousness and even a feeling of inferiority?

As a starting point, the (English) language is not proof of intelligence. It does not define people's character or do full justice to a person's competencies, so you should not see yourself as inferior to someone simply because you are less skilled in their mother tongue. Second, a conversation may only end up as good as our expectations. When we hold the pre-conceived notion that we should come off as presentable, well-spoken and competent, it already feels like a show-ground, rather than giving us 'aha' moments and the sheer joy from dialogues flowing spontaneously. This perspective flows from common observations at networking functions that connect job candidates, employers, salesmen and business persons to their prospects. As a young professional, I can totally relate to the reservations and imposter syndrome common within new-starters and candidates when

MULTILINGUAL CONNECTORS

interacting with the more senior and experienced. Naturally, we tend to treat these people courteously and considerately given their status and influence and sometimes more than necessary. It is important to note though, that our communication habits send signals to other people projecting where we place them and ourselves in the relationship in the moment and future, including but not limited to your selection of words, body language, attire, tonality and voice.

Apart from spreading distancing energy to who you interact with, being overly cautious and deliberate can also prevent you from being able to make an impression on the person you're trying to connect with, which often involves you to step further from your comfort zone and to take a little bit of risk. How many times have you ended up not asking questions not only due to your language skills but also your other reservations? For example, did you ever assume that with your experience and status, you may not deserve the support from a busy company leader? Do you even dread engaging in small talk with such individuals to explore each other as a person?

However you admire someone for their achievements and competencies, you must ground your awe or reverence to that person in reality. No one is perfect or competent in all areas. In this spirit, I firmly believe each of us can bring value in a relationship despite seniority and any other external factors that create power imbalances or feelings of inferiority initially. It makes a lot of difference to remember no one can absolutely be out of your league and hence out of your reach in all respects. This way, we could humanise the conversations in professional settings, effectively by viewing each other as real human beings who do make mistakes and need others' support from time to time.

You don't need to be 100% to give 100%

Thousands of professionals worldwide are struggling to crack the glass ceiling where they are susceptible to being passed over and undervalued for better opportunities due to their non-native speaking background. A Harvard Business Review article highlighted that non-native speakers were overall 16% less likely to be recommended for managerial positions than equally qualified native speakers. Though a range of socio-political factors contribute to this glass-ceiling effect, it is worth noting that the confidence gap does not just exist in the external context where some native speakers lack confidence about their non-native colleagues' interpersonal communication ability. An American business English training institute also revealed many non-native English speakers who are promising candidates for leadership training will opt out of participating because they face a confidence gap within themselves. Moreover, in the professional realm, such feeling is typically magnified for those who are highly educated, who possess highly technical knowledge and have a track record of professional success.

After spending months and years immersed in a foreign language environment, do you still feel too unconfident to actively participate in meetings, calls, presentations and networking where you usually cannot comprehend others and express yourself 100% clearly? Do you feel as though you are not cut out for speaking foreign languages whatsoever, which is costing you opportunities? Have you been keeping the status quo and holding yourself back from showing up in situations where you could

MULTILINGUAL CONNECTORS

be gaining opportunities, despite the nagging thought that you would deserve greater recognition and remuneration were it not for the language barrier? On the same thought, the missed opportunities as a result of your self-doubt and reservation should have also jumped to mind, especially those missed forever. As you dedicated yourself to preparing for the 'right time', you kept feeling as though you were not enough and never had the chance to make the decision for the same opportunity again. The vicious circle self-perpetuates.

> *"Do not wait: the time will never be "just right". Start where you stand, and work with whatever tools you may have at your command and better tools will be found as you go along."* — Napoleon Hill

Like many of you, at various stages of improving English overseas, I resorted to self-help resources to deal with perfectionism and imposter syndrome. I eventually learnt the hard way to embrace the wisdom of Napoleon Hill. I used to believe I would feel more confident if I could unlock another level of growth and achievement. And yes, I did. My grades were top of the faculty each year, outperforming many domestic students who I believed had many advantages in my field. I landed an industry job halfway during my bachelor's degree in Australia. I won the elections in the student union to be an officer and later on, the first non-native female president in a university society. At the outset of these opportunities, I rarely felt adequate enough and was also embodying a diminished self-image where I would assume a native speaker would fare much better. I was also very self-conscious and sensitive about how others would perceive me and therefore held myself to high performance standards. Along the journey, I realised that doubt was always part of the game and is always going to be, as long as I strive towards something greater than what I already have at the edge of my comfort zone and beyond. If a goal does not make me feel stretched and doesn't elicit feelings of self-doubt for a single moment, it is possibly not really meaningful and worth pursuing.

In coming to terms with going after greater endeavours without being 100% ready, I also gradually lived in greater harmony with the fear of judgement and rejection. I learnt and now often ask myself one key question when I'm on the verge of taking action:

Am I allowing my fear of other people's opinions to stop me from giving this opportunity a go? How bitter will I feel if someone I've deemed less qualified than myself gets rewarded for taking the risk I was too scared to take?

As a non-domestic candidate also facing financial pressures to finish my degrees in a timely manner and ideally supported by scholarships and decent jobs in Australia, I hardly felt entitled and would see most opportunities that came my way as now or never. There was nearly no option to overthink and sabotage these opportunities. Each day counted when I was on a temporary visa and could not see the end of the tunnel to settle on my dream land. With such a mentality, I firmly believed I would regret inaction much greater than any imperfect action. Compared to maxing myself out beyond the comfort zone during volunteering, working and managing academic pressures simultaneously, I knew I would feel even more uncomfortable if I was to graduate

MULTILINGUAL CONNECTORS

with a blank CV and no offer for a decent permanent job.

We don't always need to be 100% ready to give 100%, as waiting for absolute readiness or perfection will result in you never reaching the next level. For the exact same reason, the fear of inadequacy and judgement never virtually disappears even as you become more resourceful and successful. Rather than criticizing yourself for the feelings, you could embrace them as the cue to reflect on that question: do you fear more about the consequences of action, or those from inaction resulting in missed opportunities?

Having self-awareness on your strengths and limitations is vital to taking calculated risks. Yet all too commonly, people tend to focus on the risks instead of the possible gains, and let themselves ruminate on their weaknesses as a way of convincing themselves they aren't competent enough to simply make a moderate change to their skills or mindset. When I make decisions with a strong focus on the opportunity costs caused by inaction, I am easily reminded of how much meeting the target would mean to me if I chose to embrace discomfort and confront the unknown.

Such an empowering mental model paved my way to becoming the youngest tutor in the faculty when I was doing my master's. Whenever I feel inadequate in my second language nowadays, I lean into one of my most vulnerable moments: the first hour of my first face-to-face tutorial. As nervousness was striking, I took a selfie with my new title in the backdrop. In the same breath, rather than preparing my delivery, I spent way more time preparing myself. Previously, without years of industry experience under my belt or native-like English fluency, I had taken the plunge and gone beyond expectations. My skill set never rendered me 100% ready especially in regards to speaking impromptu in English, but it also never really failed me in getting things done. And I was convinced they wouldn't this time, because at least I'd studied the subject already and got decent enough grades to know what to teach someone else. I reminded myself that the professor had hired me in recognition of our collective experience in the university. In many other regards, I wouldn't have appeared a prime candidate. Yet my professor saw the potential in me, so why shouldn't I trust in myself? I also recalled how much I wished to learn in the exact same subject – how to find my feet in the construction industry. Now the ball was in my court to impart the subject content and speak from experience, but with no background of privilege. There, I came to terms with not being fully prepared, one more time. Rather than viewing tutoring as a demanding job that strained my mental muscles, it was an invaluable opportunity to give back to my successors in the community that developed me.

There is a game-changing difference between waiting for a 100% perfect moment, and making 100% of the opportunity presented in front of you. Such a tremendous difference starts well before any opportunity comes along. It starts with you believing in yourself. Stop criticising yourself for feeling not confident enough or worrying much about what others think of you. The key is, you must care about what you want way more than you do about rejection, judgement and criticism. This way, even if you do get negative results, your desire for reaching the goal can still fuel you up to move forward and show up again and again.

Such an inner motivation is a hedge against backsliding into inaction mode and the depleting stigma around your language skills or any other perceiving shortcomings.

'A GOAL PROPERLY SET IS HALFWAY REACHED.'

Many of you would have left your home countries with dreams and ambitions to pursue a better life and you should appreciate the importance of goal setting in getting you so far. Human beings are innately goal-seeking creatures built to solve problems and conquer our environments. If you do not know what you want to accomplish in the first place, it is not possible to create a plan to get there.

It is also possible to accomplish one goal after another but to still not genuinely feel you have got exactly what you want out of life. You may have got permanent residency in your host country, landed a decently paid professional job and established your own family there but still feel unfulfilled and undervalued from time to time. Conversely, you may have some idea about what you want to experience and feel in life but no clue what to do to bring them into fulfilment. Perhaps you always know you want to build close and real friendships with people from other cultures with whom you can advance your career and spend quality time with after work, yet you don't know how else to become more interpersonally effective other than improving your foreign language ability.

Tony Robbins once contended that often the actual goal is what gets in the way of achievement. If you ever struggle to live up to your goals, you can learn a critical solution in the last part of this chapter.

Means vs end goals

Some people believe they can't accomplish what they really want because they are not capable enough. In fact, many don't recognize that the failure to achieve what one truly desires is in fact often a result of confusing means goals and end goals. As will be further explained below, neither one is inherently superior to the other or right or wrong. When applied in the right way, both means and end goals are instrumental to building meaningful connections in your non-native language.

Means goals are the goals you strive for in order to accomplish your end goals. They are the stepping stones to something greater. For example, picking up more professional vocabulary and industry jargon may enable you to express yourself better in social interactions. As you communicate effectively in a language, you may have a better chance of connecting with other people, which may then attract better opportunities and relationships, which in turn improves your sense of achievement, self-worth and mental well-being, as the end goals that will be explained below.

Since goals are the vehicles that help you approach the destination, you should closely evaluate their effectiveness overtime. This is because the utility of means goals lies in their ability to produce the results you want in the envisaged timeframe. Given this, you must be flexible about them and adjust them as needed to achieve your higher objectives. In the previous example, if advancement in your non-native language still does not improve your interpersonal effectiveness in foreign settings, then you will

MULTILINGUAL CONNECTORS

need to re-examine your strategy and channel your efforts in other directions such as human psychology and other communication essentials, which a large part of this book is about.

End goals are vague and more like a direction rather than a destination. Often, they are associated with the feelings and emotional states that you wish to last for as long as possible. For example, sometimes people tend to stay in touch with those they feel a personal connection with, rather than just somebody who could advance their career. While you need to keep flexible with the means and methods to achieve your end goals, you should be more affirmative about your end goals and never compromise on the ultimate goals such as happiness, health and love. End goals should generally be non-negotiable.

It may appear to you that to master a foreign language fits with the definition of end goal because it makes you feel fulfilled and boosts your confidence. I fully respect and relate to this sentiment which renders it a desirable destination, although after a deeper reflection, I would label language acquisition as a means goal. Whilst I recall feeling a strong sense of accomplishment when I could gradually watch English TED talks without looking at subtitles all the time on my way commuting, in these moments I would envisage experiencing the better flow in conversations with foreigners in real life and feeling more secure and confident in the process. When I learnt new vocabulary on my daily commute, I would envision getting better grades for my essays in a bridging course which would qualify me for my dream university in Melbourne. When I was speaking English to myself during my showers at my Chinese homestay, I could not stop picturing myself speaking more confidently in the class presentations and social events and feeling more confident. Years later, I had upgraded my competence and confidence for public speaking at industry associations and knew the speaking engagement itself was not the end goal. In the same context, the end goal should be gaining a sense of reward from imparting my story to inspire my peers and making new connections with the prospect of adding value to each other's trajectory. In this light, as a means goal itself, improving in a language is often an enabling step to other means goals, which will inevitably propel you towards the end goals.

Often, people confuse the means with the end and have difficulties in attaching means goals to end goals which they, in the first instance, do not define properly. This way, they can sometimes get lost down the track about why they are doing what they are doing in an effort to pursue what they think they may want. This happens typically when the means is mistakenly conceived as an end or final destination itself. For instance, hundreds and thousands of non-native speakers intensively study English to get the desired scores in mainstream English tests such as IELTS and TOFEL, which are vital to live and study in an English-speaking country. When they pass the tests and get their university offers and visas, they may drop off the routine of language learning and adopt a more passive approach to it. Another example is that many university graduates become much less motivated to attend networking once they have secured a full-time job because they believe they do not need someone to connect them to good opportunities. Whilst language learning and networking both conform to the definition of means goals, some people fail to identify all the ends they could achieve via these means to sustain their motivation and action.

MULTILINGUAL CONNECTORS

Self-image and goals go hand-in-hand

Before looking at how to effectively set goals to ensure you achieve them, you must be reminded that your self-image also creates an invisible barrier to accomplishment. According to Dr. Maxwell Maltz, renowned as the grandfather of self-help books and author of *Psycho-Cybernetics,* the cybernetics mechanisms in our minds will trigger behaviours that prevent you from achieving your goals when you consider undertaking a task or challenge which is not consistent with your self-concept.

As a simple example, you are less likely to apply for a job if you cannot first see yourself meeting the criteria, long before the hiring manager gets involved. Imagine the non-native speakers who can see themselves speaking confidently in their non-native tongues, versus those who constantly picture themselves struggling in front of people and feeling embarrassed about making mistakes. In fact, the underrepresented population, such as immigrants, in many industries are reportedly more likely to experience overqualification than non-immigrants, when their level of education is higher than what is typically required for the role. While there are external factors at the cause, the same population are also prone to underrate their eligibility and competitiveness in the market to compete with their native counterparts.

Many people do not fully recognize their self-concept and its relationship with their life results. They let the historical results determine their self-concept and goals rather than redesigning their goals around a redefined self-image. Therefore, before you set any big goals and take on new challenges and risks, you must examine your self-image and make sure it is one that enables you to accomplish what you want.

DAISY WU

Because your connections won't exist without the most powerful creator of these relationships – the person who is reading.

CHAPTER 3

THE LANGUAGE YOU MUST MASTER TO MASTER ANYTHING

"Words matter. And the words that matter most are the ones you say to yourself." — David Taylor-Klaus

Provided the core idea of the last chapter, the opening quote should speak to you. Understanding your own thoughts and behaviours have a direct bearing on your performance, you must be very mindful of what you say to yourself because somebody critically influential in your life results is listening. You!

The common term in psychology for the language that defines the way you talk to yourself is self-talk, also known as your inner voice. As the name indicates, it is your internal dialogue that reflects your thoughts, beliefs, questions and ideas. It is such a critical element that David James identifies it as 'a conversation with the universe'. Self-talk is the exact language your brain uses to interpret and process daily experiences which have a profound influence on what life brings to you in all aspects. Research demonstrates positive self-talk can advance your general well-being and confidence, which in turn boosts your attention, motivation and performance. It could help one reframe stressful situations and tackle challenges more productively. An article in Healthline revealed self-talk may help athletes with endurance or to power through heavy lifting. There is also rich evidence showing people who talk to themselves in a positive manner are more likely to attain goals, score well in tests, perform better at work, recover from diseases and build good relationships.

Since the language you are scripted in has great potential to improve your life, you must have a proper command of it before you seek mastery of any area of your life to pursue your goals, whether in your native tongue or foreign language. In this chapter, I will introduce some guiding principles for you to master self-talk.

YOU ARE WHO YOU THINK YOU ARE

The way you script your inner dialogue mirrors how you perceive yourself based on what you know about yourself, which is termed as self-concept. According to Carl Rogers, an early pioneer of positive psychology, self-concept has three core parts: self image, self esteem and ideal self. Self image or real self, which was introduced in the chapter before, relates to how you currently view yourself. Self esteem is defined by the degree to which you value yourself. Ideal self is your dreams and wishes about who you want to be. Rogers believed all human beings have an inherent need to

MULTILINGUAL CONNECTORS

grow and realise their potential in the pursuit of happiness and fulfilment, which is impacted by a healthy self-concept. One of the key driving factors is congruence, as determined by how much your real self aligns with your ideal self to grow a positive and stable self-esteem. In other words, if you constantly see your current self as far behind the person you desire to be, you will hurt your ego and perpetuate negative self-talk and in turn, the negative conducts, experiences and results. With a more positive and stable sense of self, you have a better chance of coping more effectively with life's challenges with greater confidence.

Although the 2021 edition of the EF English Proficiency Index (EPI) has revealed English skills rising across multiple countries and all age cohorts, the lack of social confidence among foreign language learners at different levels is evident from the nearly 170 million search results on Google for 'speak confident English'. The fear of inadequacy and judgement haunts many people regardless of how proficient and skilled they objectively are. In this backdrop where you may identify a part of yourself, it is important to recognize the circumstances in your life are the by-product of your self-talk. On this merit, the struggles in another language are only the effect rather than the cause of your problems. I am sure you could recall numerous occasions where you've hesitated before accepting good opportunities, which ultimately resulted in you never getting that passed up opportunity presented to you ever again. You may have pulled out of doing a presentation on behalf of your team despite your instrumental contribution to the project. Perhaps you ended up avoiding a conversation with someone you admire and share common interests with during networking. Maybe you have deemed yourself unready to take on a managerial role because you weren't experienced in leading a cross-cultural team and did not really know how to do it. Or, you may simply feel nervous about meeting a new client with whom your communication styles are not familiar to each other. Understanding the influence of self-concept in these scenarios, you are more than likely to end up with missed opportunities and rejections, both actual and perceived, that validate and reinforce a diminished self-image and self-esteem: meaning you may see yourself a foreigner who is unconfident and interpersonally incompetent and therefore become stagnated and marginalised.

To improve the status quo, merely fixing the symptoms and not addressing the root cause/s is going to encourage the same issue to recur and will not sustain any positive changes. In the above example, improving language proficiency or accumulating relevant work experience will not sustainably provide the confidence and courage you need when you are scripted in fear and self-doubt. The reason for this is because our actions follow our feelings, which are a consequence of our thoughts. Thoughts originate from the mindset and belief systems they are wired in, which dictate the way you think and act. On the subject of your self concept and inner voice, to permanently treat the problem instead of temporarily mitigating the symptom, you must realise your mind is at the root of your problem. The great personal development legend Tony Robbins once famously said, 'Success is 80% psychology and 20% mechanics.' This notion of the 80-20 split between mindset and skill set in an individual's growth and development may sound familiar but there are way more people who appreciate the importance of mindset compared to those who truly understand how the mind works, which I will explain next.

How You Always Attract What You Think

"If you correct your mind, the rest of your life will fall into place." — *Lao Tzu*

As the translation of your conscious thoughts and unconscious beliefs and biases, your self-talk (which is influenced by your self-concept) originates from your mind. According to Dr Caroline Leaf who's spent over thirty years researching the mind-brain connection, thinking is the activity of the mind which works through the brain.

The mind functions on two levels, the conscious and subconscious. To help you understand, picture yourself as the image below:

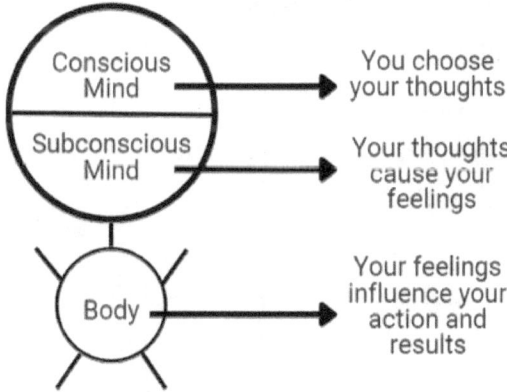

How Your Mind Works (Credit: Proctor Gallagher Institute)

At the top level is your conscious mind which registers what you hear, see, smell, touch and taste. All information from your outside world enters your consciousness via these five senses. The conscious part of your mind thinks and reasons and accepts or rejects ideas that either originate in the conscious mind itself or enter from your outside world. It is crucial to understand your conscious mind's function – which allows you to choose what to think. Once you accept a thought, whether it relates to confidence, abundance, joy, affection, fear, pain, anger or scarcity, it will be impressed upon your subconscious mind. In the above illustration, just picture your thoughts as drips of water that trickle down from the top to the level below which is the subconscious. Unless you choose to pump them out from your conscious mind or reject their entrance in the first instance, these ideas and beliefs will seep through the permeable barrier illustrated as a line between the conscious and subconscious part of the mind.

The subconscious mind is your feeling mind which generates and stores your beliefs, values, self-concept and habits, or programming as the collective term. This part has no ability to reject any thought your conscious mind chooses to accept. When the same thoughts and feelings are impressed upon your subconscious mind again and again, they will be embedded and become habitual. Without any conscious thought, you start thinking, feeling and acting in ways corresponding to your programming which is constantly subjected to the dynamics in your conscious mind. As a typical example, you may begin entertaining the notion of yourself being prone to difficulties in socialising as a foreigner even before someone expresses this opinion about you in real life. Since your subconscious cannot tell whether this idea is rational or realistic, if you frequently think and accept this belief either from your thoughts or external feedback, you will end up believing this evaluation around your interpersonal competency unconditionally. It becomes the default programming in the subconscious mind.

At the bottom of the image, your body is a visible and physical representation of you which acts as the channel via which the mind expresses itself in your words, decisions and actions which determine your results. Unless you fix and realign how you think consciously and feel subconsciously, you cannot effectively create permanent changes in your life outcomes. The reason is because our actions follow our feelings, which are a consequence of our thoughts. Thoughts, as explained earlier on, originate from the way you view the world and yourself. You must go back to your roots to examine your self-concept and worldview.

Be the person in your mind before real life

For many, it would sound more realistic that the collective experience of rejections, failures or social embarrassment shape your self-talk and establish you are not cut out for learning a foreign language or thriving interpersonally. However, have you ever wondered whether it could be who you see yourself as which causes you to behave in a way that results in these negative experiences? Does the concept strike you that by simply identifying as a sociable and confident individual, your behaviour and results will transform to align with your new identity?

In *Atomic Habits*, author James Clear discusses how changing your identity helps you build long-lasting habits for positive life results. In Clear's famous model of the 'Three Layers of Behaviour Change', he identifies your identity to be at the core or first level, which is followed by your actions (processes) and then outcomes. Provided a better understanding of how the mind works, you should now appreciate true behaviour change is really identity change. That is, you must think as if you were already the person you aspire to be for it to consciously and subconsciously guide you to alter your behaviours that are conducive to generating outcomes to construct the desired identity in real life.

Many people alter their behaviours and actions as the first step for change but often, it either fails to work or only solves the problem temporarily. As an example, expanding vocabulary on a topic might give you a surge of verbal confidence in certain contexts which comes from an increased sense of preparedness and possibly illusion of knowledge. Yet, you may still eventually revert back to withholding yourself from stepping out without addressing the inner voice which generates the behavioural patterns trapping you in the constant feeling of incompetence and inadequacy. If you cannot visualise yourself socialising confidently, and you never consciously feed your mind with the notion that you are a confident individual with strong people skills, you may start to avoid showing up at events or meetings which would've allowed you to practise and apply what you've learnt. Even if you do make your way to the meet-ups and be prepared, you may not easily grow into the habit of approaching people proactively or leading conversations where you want them. So long as it feels impossible to even imagine yourself behaving this way, the hard-wired self-image in your subconscious mind will send signals to your brain to interrupt and derail you every time you have the initiative and chance to speak up and connect with others.

Typically, the unconducive narratives in our headspace,

MULTILINGUAL CONNECTORS

otherwise known as head trash, are a combination of negative self-evaluation (e.g. 'my ideas won't sound interesting', 'I cannot nail the story in my non-native language.') or pre-emption of bad scenarios (e.g. 'People might think I'm awkward or overconfident', 'it would be inconvenient for them to provide support'). Your subconscious programming will generate passive narratives corresponding to your beliefs to talk yourself out of taking action in your own interest. This phenomenon is also known as self-sabotage, when people do or fail to do things that undermine their success or prevent them from achieving their goals. Your internal dialogue is just like a magic spell or invisible hand pulling you back despite how hard you want to forge ahead. Unfortunately, far too many people, without understanding the principles of mind mechanics and identity-based habits, let behaviours and outcomes influence their self-concept instead of conditioning their mind to fix the root cause of their bad habits.

If you are still incredulous about the above concepts and principles, I will give you my own example outside the foreign context to further illustrate. Before studying in an English-speaking country, I had low verbal confidence in both English and my first language. In the Chinese literature classes, I would be nervous when asked to read aloud, repeat after the teacher or recite. My heart would skip a beat whenever the teacher cued me sitting in the front row. For nine out of ten times I would just stutter or mumble even though I understood the learning content well. As a student council committee member, I had to give a speech in front of all the students from time to time. In my native tongue and with a script in hand, I was too nervous to increase the volume and project my voice to be heard clearly.

DAISY WU

My speech was packed with unnatural pauses and self-corrections which made me feel even more embarrassed in everyone's stare. It was mortifying to be reminded that I was made a candidate and elected in the student council primarily because of academic merits, a default criteria where I grew up studying. Meanwhile, my colleagues' feedback pretty much validated this self-evaluation, for I would always get critical comments around my social confidence in sharp contrast with solid academic records. I was top of the class but conducted myself in such a diminished way as though I were a flunker or bad-behaving student on the verge of expulsion. You can bet similar dynamics precipitated my English subjects where the speaking practice was significantly more limited.

In school, I would score off the charts in the written exams of both languages that included essay writing, but I was always frustrated and hopeless about speaking in front of others as if I was born untalented or deficient. The identity of 'the shy dux who cannot read aloud' was quite stigmatising. Without knowing the mechanisms of self-image, I could hardly tell where it was first conceived. All I remember is that before and during the class, I'd already started imagining being cued to speak and failing to nail it, just to accelerate the anxiety. I pretty much internalised that limiting self-image and constantly entertained it in the headspace, which perpetuated the results even more. Mind you, in my earlier life, there was no such thing as language or cultural barrier as a potential social challenge, but I still suffered from negative self-talk. If you are taught to or choose to believe you are not enough, most likely you will keep believing and behaving in ways that attract the results that perpetuate what you have always believed. Unless you recognize and understand the underlying pattern, you will hardly break free from the vicious cycle.

See the world as a source of support, not judgement

I was resolute about turning over a new leaf and reinventing my identity after moving to Australia, my dream land to evolve into someone who could socialise with greater confidence, especially in English. Nonetheless, for quite a while, I would always think my English was not good enough so others would not easily like or accept me and it would impact my studying and career where English was the predominant language, and I turned out to be exactly right! How so?

I often assumed I would be rejected due to my English skills, so I did not even bother asking and others hardly noticed I was keen for good opportunities so they left me out, therefore nobody was introducing me to possible industry contacts. I diminished my energy with nervousness and anxiety, so I did not come off as energised and as expressive as I should. I usually shut my mouth to avoid judgement or conflict, so I was seen as beyond introverted and very indifferent. I saw myself as less capable than those with better English, so others felt even more distant from me, being too polite and shy. As I let these results guide my behaviour, I kept attracting the same results and almost concluded I was socially awkward. 'People will not like me using imperfect English' almost became a self-fulfilling prophecy. I was right because it was never my language skills that hindered me from bonding with other people. It is how I used to see myself which affected how I behaved and generated the exact results I had expected, just like how things worked in my school years in China.

When I was trapped in a mental prison, I couldn't cognize the fundamental issues stemming from my mindset. To put it this way, I co-existed with a diminished self-image and unhealthy self-talk for a very long time before writing this book. Despite what I accomplished in an English-speaking country, I quite frankly felt haunted by the self-sabotaging thoughts and could see myself in an ongoing battle with imposter syndrome which kept resurfacing, even at the point of achievements. From this standpoint, by no means do I intend to call for more people including you to grow confidence day by day. Realistically, your confidence can go up and down depending on situations and your state of mind, which also fluctuates as a natural condition of human beings. What is critical to know is how to pick yourself up and check back in every single time your confidence drops and fear gets the better of you. As a matter of fact, simply knowing this nurtures a positive outlook and self-image where you are not only self-sufficient but well supported by the external references which constantly feed your conscious mind with information and ideas.

'Your English is quite good! I'm very impressed to find out you've only been in Australia for a few years.' I am lucky because in real life, I have literally heard a comment as such more than once from my early years in Australia. Initially it sounded too good to be true for it to register in my belief system, as I tended to consider it as nothing more than kind words of encouragement rather than a genuine compliment, in most cases from someone native-speaking in English. Notwithstanding the noises from my inner world, nobody ever realistically gave negative comments to

MULTILINGUAL CONNECTORS

my English communication, in contrast to the earlier experience in my home country. When expressed in words, the feedback turned out almost always positive and assuring, regardless of how I would evaluate my language skills. Overtime, these words of affirmation from people of different backgrounds talked louder than my inner voice as they entered my ears and echoed in my headspace.

I was always self-conscious as a Chinese immigrant and aware that my appearance and communication habits would more or less make my social image obvious and predictable. Nonetheless, at one point I decided to give others the benefit of the doubt and chose to take their compliment as heartfelt and well-intended – as they should have all actually been. I did not readily pivot to believe my English was good enough, but I at least began to embrace the idea that others were unlikely to tune me out or consider me as less than simply because I was not a native speaker of a dominant language, just like many other immigrants in the same country. Gradually, this emerging belief integrated in my behaviour as I let myself follow my curiosity to ask questions to learn from others and tell them where I came from and how I was finding life in Australia. In every attempt to express myself in English, I did not intentionally do this to impress others or to attract more nice feedback to reinforce this bettering outlook, though I practically did, as I enjoyed the process of meeting and connecting with people from different cultural backgrounds. It is certainly not just my fluency or accent that magically improved faster without practising hard on my own. In my mind's eyes, I could see myself as equal and welcome in the presence of the person I talked to. I also found myself naturally presenting myself in more open and positive body languages as well as calm and welcoming facial expressions. In that state of mind, I could stay calm and more easily recall the vocabulary and frame sentences with decent grammar when speaking impromptu but almost stressless – I would've still sounded like a non-native speaker if I'd recorded myself but in the process, I really felt in the flow and in my element.

In all honesty, I would describe my younger self in Australia as someone too lucky because without consciously regulating my beliefs and upgrading my self-image since growing up I was extremely susceptible to the passive responses from the outside world where I identify as foreign – a bad English presentation score would pretty much have done the job! From my experience and lessons, whilst you cannot 100% control what other people say to you, you do and should have 100% control of what to keep within and out of your mind space. Your conscious mind listens to your subconscious mind and acts without judging! The continually repeated words will be translated in the subconscious mind as affirmations, either positive or negative, even if the person saying it didn't mean it, either you or someone else. Whatever your outlook is about how others treat you from your interpretation of their behaviours in your conscious mind, after some time, it becomes a part of your subconscious conditioning as your key reference when your ego takes a hit in the face of failures and setbacks. To rescript the narrative that defines your worldview and coping mechanisms, you must reposition yourself appropriately. In other words, you should revisit and re-examine your self-image. It all starts from you.

MULTILINGUAL CONNECTORS

IT GETS EASY WHEN YOU CARE ENOUGH

Motivation is one of the most important execution skills and arguably one of those which many people are challenged to develop. Apart from the anticipated feeling of indebtedness, the fear of rejection and judgement often makes us hold off outbound communications: asking for support, applying to opportunities, leaning in to connections, etc. I've come across plenty of motivational content emphasising the cost of inaction to propel people, in the backdrop of overcoming fear to take action. Even with the focus shifting from the risks of action to the consequences of inaction, fear remains a dominant emotion governing our behaviours. In my opinion, it is not sustainable to be scripted in 'FOMO' (Fear of Missing Out) in the constant feeling of apprehension that one is missing out on information, events, experiences, or life decisions which can improve one's status quo.

For one thing, it takes quite a lot of mental energy to keep the gesture as a 'fear warrior'. Not only do we entertain the negative outcomes of our actions, we also pre-empt the scenarios where we get stuck, lag behind and miss out due to the action not taken. Remember, our mind has the powerful function of imagination. Yet oftentimes we are also prone to stretch our imagination in the negative direction, especially when there is little personal reference to support the benefits of action. It is emotionally draining to contemplate and take action with fear fuelling your imagination. Keep doing this and you will eventually be paralysed into inaction by the emotional and psychological response of fear, which, based on research evidence, can numb your emotions and thoughts, resulting in poor decisions and judgments.

Moreover, it is key to note our actions are driven by our feelings. Our feelings are a byproduct of our thoughts which stem from the mindset belief system. Given this, in order to improve your ability of execution, there is something more powerful to replace fear as the key motivator to execute and to deal with the fear over action: what you truly care about as the reward of the action taken. If you remember how the mind works, it is possible to reorient your beliefs and condition your mind to believe in the potential reward of your action even at a scale more than it realistically could be. Once you are so convicted about the anticipated rewards which can arouse positive feelings like being proud and excited, you will naturally be motivated into action despite the perceived risks. As soon as you gain some form of reward from execution, a positive circle begins to reinforce your beliefs around the benefit of taking calculated risks and to sustain positive behaviour The reward at the beginning can be as small but substantial as a joyful conversation experienced during networking without it leading to a job or deal, to keep you motivated to attend the next one with a positive outlook.

You will have trouble mustering what it takes to ask for what you want, subjecting yourself to rejection, judgement and criticism, unless you really care about what you are asking for. I actually learnt the power of caring from my family who visited Australia several times to help me settle better into my new life. Barely knowing any English, they would have to access somebody else bilingual to find their way around and do shopping when I was in school. Occasionally, they also needed a translator to do bigger problem-solving such as finding a plumber and liaising

MULTILINGUAL CONNECTORS

with the concierge. Whilst there were many Chinese-Asians in the neighbourhood, I could imagine the additional practical challenges to navigate a foreign environment besides the language. Their bias for action and problem-solving skills turned out to be remarkably beyond my imagination despite all barriers. 'There's no other way ... I must figure things out without bothering you when you are attending your class. Everyday I need to bring something to the table and your lunch box ... ' Where we lived, there was always a likelihood that they would approach someone Chinese-looking but find out they were unable to assist my family in translation for all sorts of reasons. I always knew they wanted to take good care of my daily chores to allow me to focus on studying and making new friends here. They cared about looking after me in our home away from home so much that they would adapt themselves in the new environment by any means necessary.

Compared to my family, back then I was much more hesitant to ask for assistance whether it was big or small, even though I could command the English language relatively well for at least the basic functional support. Somehow, unlike my family with almost nothing to lose when reaching out to strangers in a foreign land, I could see myself bearing a certain level of emotional and social risks when interacting with friends and acquaintances. I tended to be self-conscious, overthink a lot and pre-empt rejection. I worried about troubling and bothering others. So what did it take for me to transform into the more action-oriented and go-getting person who maximises the opportunities on her radar?

From struggling to ask for directions, to sitting down with a friendly native-speaking colleague after an awkward first few minutes at my first pub drink in college, to unexpectedly getting a job referral after promoting events in lectures, I tasted the functional and emotional rewards that outweighed the risks to make it all worth the initial qualm and discomfort. Moreover, as I expanded my dedication to leading volunteering ventures to support people like me on social integration and professional development overseas, action bias became more and more of a must and slowly became second nature. As I stretched my comfort zone through public speaking, pitching for collaboration and leading meetings, most of the time I was actually interdependent rather than independent in converting and executing opportunities. 'The apple doesn't fall far from the tree.' There I saw myself shadowing my family in Australia, where we cared about and asked for what we needed regardless of the risks. It is my belief that such a quality should've always been within me, but had been dormant in the earlier phase where there didn't seem to be something I cared immensely about that outweighed the feeling of vulnerability. Referencing back to my family visiting Melbourne, they cared incredibly about the outcomes which mattered to somebody they cared for, namely me. In the same measure, when the volunteering projects took off and those watching the space provided positive feedback and appreciative notes, the only voice in my head was 'I would do this again next time and do more' which spoke louder than the NOs from the inner and outside world.

When you care, you upgrade the inner dialogue from 'I have to do X so that I won't feel or experience something negative as a result of not achieving Y' to 'I get to do X so that I will be rewarded with the positive feelings upon achieving Y'. The power of execution will sustainably fuel you from inside out when you are driven by care rather than from outside in, when you are ruled by fear.

A GREAT ATTITUDE OF THE HEART

The great Zig Ziglar described gratitude as the 'healthiest of all human emotions' and 'the most important and by far the most life-changing' of all the attitudes we can acquire. When we have a feeling of gratitude, we appreciate the good aspects of things and people just the way they are. Gratitude does not only have to go towards anything big or significant. It can be anything that could seem too trivial to praise or we would have almost taken for granted.

> *"Gratitude is not only the greatest of virtues, but the parent of all the others."* — Marcus Tullius Cicero

Some people believe they must obtain their wants in order to feel gratitude. However, in practice and the great Cicero's wisdom, it is the other way around. You will get what you want if and only if you inhabit a spirit of gratitude. In Zig Ziglar's terms, the more you express gratitude for what you have, the more likely you will have even more to express gratitude for. Why?

Referring to the mind mechanics illuminated earlier in the chapter, the language of appreciation has the transformational power to shift your programming from scarcity to abundance. This is conducive to cultivating a healthy self-concept where you accept and appreciate your real self (self-image) even though it may not perfectly match who you aspire to become (ideal self). Self-appreciation comes with compassion and self-reflection. It is about getting in the habit of recognizing and acknowledging the little qualities that shape you into who you are and the small steps that lead you to where you want to be. It is also about recalling the challenges and setbacks you have already overcome and the lessons you have learnt to grow. As you deliberately practise self-appreciation, you consciously activate these memories over and over again in your subconscious. This way, it would be easier to internalise such affirmations as 'I am enough', 'I am very good but can become even better' and 'I can tackle the challenges that come my way just as I did in the past' at the subconscious level to drive behaviours for results to prove them true in a positive loop.

With a growth mindset, it is tempting to visualise ourselves constantly chasing the next best thing on the horizon with the illusion of never reaching our most desired state ever. In respect to learning a foreign language and culture, the compulsion to progress and level up can be especially strong among immigrants like many of you and myself. As such, we can easily lose perspective on our progress and the skills, qualities and character within us that enable us to achieve what we have. On the other hand, the experience of establishing life in a new environment should provide ample reference to help you regain perspective. In the experience I share above, I often needed the native-speaking counterparts to validate and remind me of how far I had come in a foreign country to achieve what the locals might take for granted. The appreciation of the person I am, shaped by my collective experience and lessons insofar, largely reinforce my confidence in the anticipation of new challenges.

MULTILINGUAL CONNECTORS

An attitude of gratitude calibrates your focus on what you are grateful for and therefore helps you concentrate on how much you already have instead of what you don't. The journey of establishing life almost from zero to one in a foreign environment provides fertile ground for gratitude to seed and flourish. A large part of it is maintaining perspective. Compared to many local citizens, I am far less likely to take things for granted or feel entitled to others' support and assistance. This is not only because I had to pay multiples times the university tuition fees a domestic student would or faced restrictive hiring policies due to visa and citizenship status. It is probably also not because I did not migrate with my family but started off as an international student in a city with barely anyone to lean on. Rather than considering myself in a scarcity-based outlook or victim mentality, external conditions and circumstances as such constantly hold me accountable for gratitude practice. This way, I seldom take rejection as personal or intuitively attribute them to my cultural origin or immigrant background. I also never accept I should settle for anything less than I deserve under the influence of conscious and unconscious bias. With gratitude, these challenges of establishing life overseas, whether true or imagined, tremendously sharpen my mind to be more alert and attuned to the positive around me in any situation.

Gratitude also prevents me from holding a sense of complacency or entitlement, for I know I could not have come as far as I have without everyone who crossed my path. I am beyond thankful for those who provided me with positive affirmations along the journey that let me put language proficiency into perspective to build the foundation of my thought leadership. I also owe lifelong appreciation to those who provided significant guidance for me to move the needles and transform my trajectory, such as the life-changing mentorship from mentors. Equally, I am grateful for the ones who showed me the way when I was lost and on the verge of missing public transport; those who listened to me with great patience, checked understandings and helped me paraphrase; those who 'liked' my earliest English social media posts to keep me motivated; those who trained me up on the job and acknowledged my contributions; even those who invited me to their tables to expand my friend circles. Such deep gratitude also motivates me to stay in touch with them and look out for opportunities to reciprocate and be a valuable asset to my much cherished connections. At any point before such an opportunity comes my way, I will make sure that these people know how appreciative I am for what they have done for me, or simply knowing and having them in my tribe.

The language of gratitude is indeed powerful and transformative and can usually be expressed in simple terms like 'thank you'. My last advice on gratitude is, don't just practise it in your inner world and express it to yourself to propel you forward. Make sure your connections can see and hear this from the outside – because words are powerful.

CHAPTER 4

DON'T WORK HARDER ON THE LANGUAGE

"Tell me and I forget, teach me and I may remember, involve me and I learn." – Benjamin Franklin

Though advancement in a language on its own does not guarantee interpersonal effectiveness when living overseas, language acquisition still requires your due regard. Even with language barrier a widely quoted challenge for certain populations, the 2021 Australian Census revealed that among roughly 30% of the population who spoke a language other than English at home and were born overseas, the majority of which rated themselves as speaking English well or very well. Note that responses to the question on proficiency in English in the census are subjective. In other words, while some people may only consider a response of 'well' as appropriate if one can hold a deep and engaging social conversation, others may put down the same response if they can simply communicate well enough to meet work demands. In light of this, the latest census data concur with the perspective which inspired me to create this chapter.

As the role of language has been discussed from multiple angles so far, it should resonate that you should not solely rely on external matrices such as language tests to gauge your competencies in commanding a language. From my standpoint and the above data, a more constructive measure of language skills is its utility. In this context, utility can be interpreted as how much your language enables you to meet the objectives behind the communication of your life situations, regardless of how you score in any objective evaluations.

While there are inevitable limits in the language curriculum and learning resources, a lot of them effectively teach people what to learn rather than how to learn. Even fewer impart how to personalise your own strategy to maximise the outputs rather than inputs of your learning, to enable you to fulfil the practical objectives, such as performing well on the job or connecting with people from other cultures.

Acknowledging the widespread notion of languages being a tool for communication, if your primary intention is to sharpen and maximise this tool to carve out better relationships and opportunities, you shouldn't have to work as hard as you would have been told in schools for various reasons you will discover in this chapter.

MULTILINGUAL CONNECTORS

THE LANGUAGE IS A LIFESTYLE, NOT A STANDALONE PRACTICE

"For the things we have to learn before we can do them, we learn by doing them." - Aristotle

The above quote by Ancient Greek philosopher Aristotle underscores the role of experiential learning whereby knowledge is created through transformation of experience. On a really basic level you are hardly going to internalise what you have learnt about the language till you actually use that language. It's about implementing what you've learnt from your everyday experiences, not just learning from textbooks.

When it comes to foreign language acquisition, interpersonal skills development and their overlay as the key subject of this book, many of you have ample opportunity to integrate experiential learning in a foreign environment. On the surface, it does appear migrants and expats have unparalleled advantages over the counterparts in their home countries. It is however evident that many people fall short of capitalising on experiential learning even with increased exposure to the target language. According to the Sydney Morning Herald, in 2018, 820,000 Australian adults from non-English speaking backgrounds lacked a decent grasp of English, compared with 300,000 in 1981. Similar trends are observed in other English-speaking countries including the U.S. A large number of learners stagnate at basic and functional levels to narrowly get through the day-to-day. Amongst those aspiring to keep advancing to integrate better in a foreign society, many, despite living in an immersive language environment, still face practical challenges in learning on their own terms after leaving school.

Many work hard to live up to their study routines around contents that may not be frequently applied to meet practical demands. For example, some people push hard to keep the routine of reading books and newspapers and listening to news and podcasts in their non-native language. Yet these people may still struggle in conversations where they barely get to implement a lot of the new vocabulary that they learn. Also, as mentioned before, regardless of such efforts that have resulted in substantial progress in language proficiency, quite a lot of people don't believe they will ever become good enough. Typically, these people display a tendency to over prepare and overthink interactions outside of their native circles.

"Insanity is doing the same thing, over and over again, but expecting different results." — Albert Einstein

Regardless of how you have been doing to improve in a foreign language, as long as you are not satisfied with the results you've been getting from learning and implementing a foreign language, it is time to stop and reflect on your current approach. To re-emphasise the idea in the subtitle, you must appreciate that motivation is overrated, if not often considered in the wrong way. To put this statement into perspective, consider that you have well passed the stage where you have to work on a language for the mere sake of survival or passing exams. By now you should recognize that real life situations are in fact the key motivator and start being able to recognise the disconnect between what you've learnt in practice and what real life demands.

In the rest of the chapter, I will introduce some principles to help you bridge this gap and become more productive and purposeful on your learning journey. Beware that I am not an English as a Second Language (ESL) teacher to impart the principles and technicalities of language acquisition. I am also not going to be highly prescriptive about what to learn and how to learn. I am here to introduce a number of time-tested productivity and performance principles to guide you to realign your targets and strategies to help be more effective and efficient on your learning journey.

PRODUCTIVITY AND PERFORMANCE PRINCIPLES

Small steps

> "Bit by bit, whatever you see to be petty becomes plenty." — Israelmore Ayivor

While long-term goals are significant in our growth and development, here I want to delve into the power of short-term goals which are often underrated and underused for sustainable performance and productivity in language acquisition. To mitigate the difficulties around translating what you learn into what you do and the other way round, here are a few strategies for you to capitalise on the advantages of short-term goals:

1. Immediate motivation: Consider how driven and disciplined you were when you were plugging away in an effort to pass

English tests so that you could go overseas and start a new life. In these scenarios, I can imagine you would have held yourself accountable given that the immediate goal (moving overseas) was conditional on the advancement in English – there was a sense of urgency. To reapply this, you should map out the short-term goals that can lead up to your long-term goals. Let's say speaking your second language confidently in the professional realm within 1-2 years is a long-term goal. Once you break down the long-term goal over the desired timeframe, you should pinpoint some small and specific targets in the short run, such as the next weekly office drink, the coffee catch-up with an acquaintance in three days and the incoming industry event. This way, you can tailor your practice and preparation to be more topical. Back to the example of reading and watching news daily, you would be more intentional and effective if you study the topic in anticipation of putting it in application as soon as possible.

2. Compound momentum: In contrast to studying for exams, the practices necessary for real-life scenarios are not once-off efforts. Rather, in the examples given above, it is far more likely that you will reapply what you have learnt instead in more meaningful and approachable short-term goals after you've reached your initial goals. What you've said or heard others say in a networking event can translate into lessons – lessons that will start to compound in similar settings in the future. This will lend itself to deliberate practice. Unlike general practice, that might include mindless repetitions with only yourself in most instances, deliberate practice is purposeful and systematic. It is conducted with the specific goal of improving performance. This is where you seek the most practical means as a way to evaluate your progress (e.g. attending a meet-up to have real-life conversations instead of just recording yourself in another language).

3. Actionable behaviour: Instead of being a long-winded way of saying 'creating motivation', actionable behaviour is the by-product of short-term goals which, compared to long-term goals, are usually much easier to formulate to be specific and measurable. It is typically easier to determine where to calibrate your focus and attention in areas of priority, an important element for deliberate practice. For instance, instead of practising listening to random selected podcasts and radios in a broad range of topics, you may benefit more from listening to the podcast interview of someone you expect to network with. I personally find this is an effective means to prepare for field- or industry-specific networking settings. Other times, each social media post I write is a self-contained short-term goal in the grand scheme of honing my English writing and expanding my productive vocabulary – which will be introduced later. Such activities are not only practical to easily integrate in my daily life, they are also well aligned in a way that they gradually become a constructive and enjoyable part of my lifestyle instead of an isolated workload or study task.

4. Self-efficacy: Short-term goals are more likely to promote self-efficacy simply because they take less time to accomplish than the long-term ones. A popular study published in Nature noted that when we set a goal for ourselves, we experience a spike of dopamine – a chemical released in the brain that makes you feel good and motivates you to take productive action. Yet we will not experience the same dopamine spike again until we are close to achieving that goal. Though dopamine bookends the pursuit of goals, its absence during the middle phase (where the essential actions are due), makes goal achievement challenging as motivation dwindles from the start. Under such a dynamic, it can be harder to manage your performance to achieve long-term goals However, you can leverage this principle to your advantage by breaking the long-term goals into a series of enabling short-term goals – which will inevitably promote a sense of self-efficacy. Each time you achieve a short-term goal, you feel rewarded in the dopamine surge and therefore more confident in your capacity to unlock more goals to sustain your motivation and action. As the general saying goes, 'Success breeds success'.

The Pareto Principle

The Pareto Principle originally referred to the observation by Italian economist Vifredo Pareto, that 80% of Italy's wealth belonged to only 20% of the population. It is now well known as the 80/20 rule, a theory maintaining that roughly 80% of consequences come from 20% of causes. The 80/20 rule asserts an unequal relationship between inputs and outputs, reinforcing the notion that it is more important to work smarter, not harder. So how can we apply the Pareto Principle to learning the language more productively?

As a starting point, assess your goals continuously. Failing to set the target right is simply like leaning your ladder against the wrong wall. No matter how hard and tall you climb, it will take much longer for you to get to where you desire. The earlier section discusses why and how to tap into the power of short-term goals to pave the way for long term goals. Within the short-term goals you have identified for a long-term goal, remember not all

MULTILINGUAL CONNECTORS

of them are equally crucial and enabling. Map out those small goals that represent the 20% that propel you through key milestones towards the destination. They are the ones that deserve most of your energy and dedication.

Secondly, you need to critically evaluate the activities frequently based on your goals. Under the Pareto Principle, 80% of your goals can be accomplished with just about 20% of the vital tasks. As you integrate language acquisition in practical settings to capitalise on experiential learning, take an inventory to identify which activities form the 20% that respond to the real-life demands as enlisted below:

Linguistic: This generally refers to the core skills commonly assessed in mainstream language tests. Though the tests have intrinsic limitations to genuinely or holistically reflect one's language proficiency in one or more competency areas, the skills frequently assessed in those tests can be your reference for this purpose. Here is a non-exhaustive list: vocabulary, grammar, oral fluency, pronunciation, written discourse, overall accuracy, speed of understanding and delivery, conversation skills.

Contextual: Take a step further from self-assessing the language skills listed above and closely examine their applications in your life situations. Specifically, what are the ones most frequently applied in your day-to-day life? What are the ones critical to accomplishing your goals?

Vocabulary learning is a key example to illustrate the application of Pareto Principle as a framework for you to determine what to learn before you seek out how to learn. Here, it would be useful to introduce the concept of productive vocabulary and receptive vocabulary. Productive vocabulary, also known as active vocabulary or working vocabulary, is the words an individual regularly uses. In contrast, receptive vocabulary, also called passive vocabulary or recognition vocabulary, refers to the words one can understand when used by others rather than the ones he or she normally uses. Given the definitions, you may tend to think the most instrumental 20% comes predominantly from productive vocabulary. Practically, though, for most people, there is an overlay of both in multiple contexts.

Also note that vocabulary learning is primarily receptive and learners are more likely to gain receptive knowledge than productive knowledge, according to a study published by Cambridge University Press. Though it is a widely accepted and researched endeavour to turn receptive vocabulary into a productive one, given the 80/20 rule, you should assess your life situations and determine where it would be best to channel your efforts. For example, if you find yourself struggling in listening and comprehension as a key task at work but are generally on top of responding in your productive language, then you may focus more on expanding your receptive vocabulary. Alternatively, if you read and listen well but often cannot find the exact word to say during conversation, your strategy will be different.

For many of you reading this book, a key priority in your language learning is functional language, which is language that you need in various day-to-day situations such as greeting, making an introduction, explaining concepts, sending requests and negotiating. Typically, functional language comprises fixed expressions. For example, to express an opinion, you could use: 'From my perspective…', 'In my view …'. Or, to give advice, you may say 'If I were you, I would … ' or 'My suggestion is …' The more functional language you master, the more real-life situations you can interact in using the target language. Similar to vocabulary learning, the 80/20 rule is also highly applicable in functional language learning.

Lastly, learning takes time so you must identify the time at which your performance and productivity peaks. How you spend time learning the language and how you learn are not the main focus here. That is, it is not of key essence whether you stick to regular time blocks to deliberately learn the language, or only do it when you have discretionary time or practise intensively on-demand. To implement the 80/20 rule, you must know when the most effective time of day is to implement your learning plan. You may identify one or a few time slots during which you are typically most productive every day or week for such cognitively demanding activities. The next step is then to optimise your schedule to accommodate the critical learning activities in as many of these prime time slots as possible. In my case, I have a daily vocabulary learning routine on a phone app and the most productive time to do it is the twenty to thirty minutes of commuting time. For social media content production which allows me to hone writing skills, I am the sharpest in the two to three hours before bedtime.

Concentrate on your strengths, not weaknesses

Do you often find it easier to list your weaknesses compared to your strengths when you talk about them?

It is common to try to hide our weaknesses from others, with language abilities being no exception. A large number of non-native English speakers in multinational firms reportedly scored high in English tests but low on the bar of confidence due to the perceived impacts of English skills. This is in spite of their advanced education, technical acumen and professional track record in their respective fields. Surely it is important to have awareness of your weaknesses, yet it is just as if not more critical to understand and appreciate your strengths. Nonetheless, if we do not understand and showcase our own strengths, we are almost left with nothing to construct our self-image. Our weaknesses start to dominate us when we fail to acknowledge our strengths. It is truly dangerous to let weaknesses cloud our decisions when we place too much emphasis on them.

Here is another thing: when you base decisions on weaknesses, you think in a passive mode in which you pick one option over the other to avoid exposing your weaknesses. This can easily create the illusion of settling for the second best or less due to your weaknesses. However, if you reframe your decision making to be governed by your strengths, you will possibly arrive at the same decision but in a significantly more positive frame of mind. You are still strategic about not taking on a task which your skill set does not well match up to. Yet you will feel more convicted about the chosen path as the best possible choice you can think of to maximise your strengths to propel you towards goals. Below are two examples to illustrate this:

Example 1:
- Weakness-oriented narrative: I decided to be responsible for preparing my group presentation content instead of delivering the presentation because my presentation skills are poor

and I have a thick accent.
- Strength-oriented narrative: I decided to be responsible for preparing my group presentation content instead of delivering the presentation because of my excellent understanding of the subject matter and ability to write well in plain language.

Example 2:
- Weakness-based narrative: I decided not to attend large professional events because I tend to get very nervous in impromptu talks with strangers and struggle to lead English conversations in a group.
- Strength-based narrative: I decided not to attend large professional events because I fare better in one-on-one catch-ups where I get more space and time to talk more intimately with the other person and can often steer the conversation better with some preparation.

It would be obvious from the above that weakness-based decision making narratives are more diminishing and demoralising, instead of being empowering and assuring. When the same action is taken in different outlooks, it can also lead to divergent results. Recalling what the earlier chapters covered about mind mechanics, the narratives lingering in your conscious mind will be impressed upon your subconscious mind to profoundly influence your behaviours and self-image over time. In turn, the two distinct outlooks will also affect how others perceive you. It is your duty to control what you register in other people's minds and make sure they remember and value you for what you are good at. Besides, as you may outgrow some of your weaknesses overtime, it is better not to leave the impression of incompetence by highlighting them and thereby killing future opportunities in the cradle.

> *"If you focus on improving the things you are already good at, you'll master the skill. Focusing only on weaknesses creates mediocrity."* — Jay Shetty

As embodied by the above quote, a philosophy subscribed by many celebrities in the self-development realm goes that if you work on your weaknesses, you will merely elevate them to a point where they are no longer weaknesses, but possibly not strengths either. Instead, exerting the same amount of effort, you may excel at the ones you are already good at. Focusing excessively on your weaknesses creates mediocrity and can turn you into a jack-of-all-trades. The complete saying associated with this term was originally 'A jack of all trades is a master of none, but oftentimes better than a master of one.' Without discounting a diversified skill set, it does highlight the danger of dabbling rather than gaining expertise in at least a few areas.

When it comes to language skill development, you should be strategic about how it is formulated by your strengths and weaknesses. Research shows people who focus on their strengths are more confident and resilient, have higher levels of energy, perform better at work and are more likely to reach their goals. Despite this, it is more common for people to work much harder to improve on their weaknesses and fail to improve on their strengths when they are not given parallel emphasis. The mainstream language tests such as IELTS seek to test an individual's

MULTILINGUAL CONNECTORS

all-rounded skills in a language, generally listening, reading, speaking and writing. While demand from exams and assessments naturally push people to plug away at their areas of weakness to pass the hurdles, in real-life you should integrate the philosophy of maximising your strengths in foreign language acquisition, especially if you are in a foreign environment.

Back in the days when you had to study for language exams, you would have been advised to be strategic in your preparation where it's impractical to literally study everything and the Pareto principle should be applied for productivity. Once you've left school, you should keep a strategic mind in your continuous learning to meet real-life demands or even better, be intentional about doing things that enable you to maximise what you are relatively good at in that language.

Unlike school exams, you should have a bit more autonomy about what to study for and what problems to solve. For instance, ideally your career choice enables you to play to your strengths within the language and beyond. It is also worthwhile examining which skills in the language you require the most to perform the 20% most value-adding activities and how much they overlap your strengths. Insofar, the book should have let you regain perspective on the role of language proficiency in human connections. Even if you see your language ability as a weakness in your overall competencies, it should not prevent you from integrating the language into the top 20% high-value skills, with the skill of connecting high in the rank. As you continuously advance in the language and hone in on the other skills critical to the 20% high-value activities, the language should always be viewed as a subset of all the core skills required.

To refine your learning strategy with a stronger focus on your strengths I suggest you assess your language skills in the following categories introduced with the 80/20 rule above:

Linguistic: Where are you strongest in some of the common skill categories in language tests: vocabulary, grammar, oral fluency, pronunciation, written discourse, overall accuracy, speed of understanding and delivery, conversation skills.

Contextual: What are the topics you feel most competent in communicating about, through writing, speaking, or both?

Ensure you do evaluate the skills in the full context on their frequency of application and relative importance. On this basis, I devised the 'Double-E' Language Learning Matrix comprising four quadrants determined by your relative proficiency in language abilities or context and its utility in real life. For each quadrant, the corresponding learning strategy is encapsulated in two 'E's, as will be explained below. Overall, these quadrants are in order of priority based on the philosophy of strengths being a focal point in growth and advancement.

The 'Double-E' Language Learning Matrix

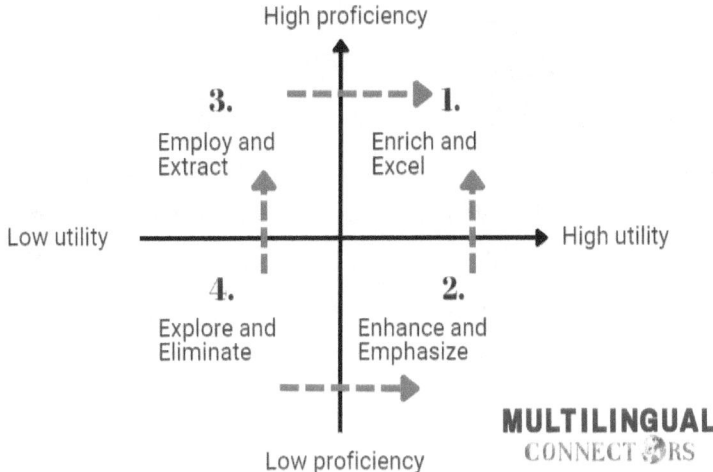

Quadrant One – high proficiency and high utility: The first quadrant represents what you are competent at and frequently use to communicate on a everyday basis in a target language. You should continuously improve on what you are already good at and maximise the opportunities to apply and in doing so advance these competencies. If you possess strong writing skills in your working field, you should consciously apply and promote your strengths in as many job tasks as possible to stand out. Besides, content writing on social media can also be an effective way to promote your writing skills and field knowledge. Based on your strengths and interests, you can also hone in on developing these skills to carve out a side hustle, such as freelance writing.

Quadrant Two – low proficiency and high utility: These are the skills which you need to focus on growing for the current and future demand in your life situations. For example, you may already know well the field specific vocabulary to perform the technical tasks at work with basic functional language primarily through writing, which belong to Quadrant One. However, these skills would have been categorized in Quadrant Two when you just started working and had to prioritize enhancing these proficiencies. Right now or in the future, to advance into a senior position, you probably need to expand your functional language along with speaking skills to present information, lead meetings, provide instructions and negotiate more frequently. Ideally, all the proficiencies in Quadrant Two you focus on improving will become your strengths in Quadrant One.

Quadrant Three – high proficiency and low utility: This quadrant captures what you have mastered in a target language but do not often employ to communicate in your current daily life. For example, you used to socialise via sports activities with your old colleagues but no longer share the same interests with anyone in your current workplace. To give another example, you got to apply your creative writing skills to fulfil the marketing committee role in a university club but your current job does not entail creative writing. The recommended strategy for Quadrant Three is similar to Quadrant One except the focus is mainly on exploring opportunities to employ and promote your proficiency, which can take form in many ways. In the previous examples, you may seek to expand your social circle outside of work with those with whom you share common interest and navigate an alternative or additional job where you can build on your skills. This can help you maintain your proficiencies through frequent usage and practice, to upgrade them into Quadrant One. Active

MULTILINGUAL CONNECTORS

application is key to enhance familiarity, which is critical to building confidence. You shouldn't always let go of what you already know well to the degree you almost forget how proficient you are or used to be.

Quadrant Four - low proficiency and low utility: This quadrant is the collective of the skills and knowledge you are both not strong in and do not usually need in your life situations at present. So long as it does not interfere with your ability to deal with most situations day to day, you can eliminate them from your learning plan by applying the 80/20 rule. For me, I've made a conscious decision to give up on sports vocabulary since I am not keen to join any sports-related activities or dialogue and feel comfortable with stepping away from this topic during social activities. In contrast, years before I was neither proficient nor immersed in the languages of the personal development realm which I employ a lot in mentoring, writing and speaking these days. With my interests growing in this area, the relevant language proficiencies became a learning priority in Quadrant Two which gradually evolved Quadrant One as I kept upskilling. Your Quadrant Four skills can also move in another direction (low proficiency and low utility >> high proficiency and low utility >> high proficiency and high utility). A personal example, I casually pick up vocabulary in musical theory and composition and occasionally go to concerts and play instruments with English-speaking friends. Possibly, one day I will become more proficient in the field specific language and this may also motivate me to engage in more activities on this hobby. As your life situations evolve, you can definitely change your learning strategies in this quadrant.

It is also instrumental to understand the correlations between your skills in order to pinpoint where to concentrate your energy and maintain perspective. In some cases a weakness is merely due to the lack of practice rather than genuine lack of talent. For example, you are highly efficient at picking up new vocabulary but fall short of professional communication due to insufficient knowledge about industry jargons because you've just entered the workforce. In this case, you can leverage your strength to bridge knowledge gaps. In the same vein, you should not discount your potential of becoming an excellent presenter simply because you didn't prepare well in your first few presentations whilst you do speak fluently and eloquently in general conditions. In addition, some weaknesses actually cap your strengths and will hinder you from improving your overall performance, such as concentration. Regardless of how hard you work on your strengths, until you deal with these weaknesses, you cannot go far. As an example, you will have difficulty in doing better at leading meetings given your low confidence level despite your solid grammar and vocabulary. Thus, you generally should not ignore your weaknesses but avoid being too obsessed with fixing them at the ignorance of your strengths. Whilst you keep working on your weaknesses, you should always focus more on maximising your strengths, in the language itself and beyond.

MULTILINGUAL CONNECTORS

NEVER WALK ALONE

> *'Independence is not supreme! Independent people who do not have the maturity to think and act interdependently may be good individual producers, but they won't be good leaders or team players.'* — Stephen Covey

To enable you to work smarter, not just harder in a non-native language, I would like to conclude this chapter with the importance of delegation. Since most of you usually do not have real-time access to an interpreter or communication expert, you should proactively think about how you can leverage others' strengths to bridge your weaknesses in the target language. You should continually be looking for people capable of doing certain parts of your work better than you, including but not limited to the use of the foreign language itself.

By definition, the concept of delegation is most frequently cited in leadership and management literature. It is vouched for given the premise of improving efficiencies, engagement and trust that can benefit the individual who delegates and other team members. Bear in mind the right of delegation is not only reserved for those in leadership and management roles, despite practical limitations. Even if you are not in a professional setting or performing any leadership or management function, it will be beneficial to you to embrace the mindset of delegation as you take full ownership and ultimate responsibility of everything you do on the job and beyond.

When I was leading at non-for-profit organisations, I would be in my element when ideating and planning initiatives as an executive committee. For publicity, it would be delegated when I felt constrained by my English and marketing language. Though I became increasingly more versed in pulling the marketing collateral, I knew someone else in the team could do it better and would generally refrain from stepping in even if I had time. Instead, I would channel my time and energy to project planning and outbound communications for partnering and sponsorship. For sure, to me and the other committees, we would not have been as effective or fulfilled had we swapped our duties.

You can still indirectly practise delegation when you have limited power and resources by looking for those who are on a similar task or have already done what you want to accomplish and who you know are more competent. You may seek general guidance or references (e.g. project template) from these people wherever practical. You should be highly considerate in your approach and respect the boundaries of those who have no obligation to assist you. Also, remember you do not necessarily need to ask for their assistance explicitly or be fully transparent about your dependence.

When initially attending industry events during university, language barriers made things even harder. As I got to know more classmates who spoke better English and were also looking for similar roles, I would invite them to attend the events together and stay with them when they were talking to professionals. Whilst my colleagues were not virtually leading the conversations on my behalf, I did benefit a lot from listening to and observing them on the side. Most of the time the conversation contents were highly relevant to me. Before my verbal confidence substantially improved in such formal settings, I would do some research

MULTILINGUAL CONNECTORS

about the participating organisations and guests and share with my colleagues what might be of interest to us to enquire more about. Often they would appreciate me for the kind gesture and remembered to ask these questions after my reminders before the function. Over time, I accumulated knowledge and vocabulary about the industry and professional networking in this manner, which eventually propelled me to participate more actively in conversations.

While delegation can empower others to apply and develop their skill sets, you should also leverage it to upskill yourself. Pay close attention to how the person you delegate the task to delivers the results better and faster. With better knowledge of other people's strategies and processes, you can either keep delegating the same task in future or work towards doing it by yourself with a refined approach. In my early career, there were ample opportunities to learn and shadow my colleagues, when I tagged along my supervisors in the meetings, stayed tuned in email loops and mingled in social functions. This also kept me better informed of others' strengths to practise delegation in future, even though I was not performing the exact tasks as I observed others doing.

The above examples of navigating language barriers in my early career speak to the critical role of interdependence, which is akin to being in a successful partnership or team. Compared to dependence and independence, it's not about 'you' or 'I' but rather it is about 'we'. Dr. Stephen Covey describes interdependence as 'the highest level of maturity' which is essential to achieve win-win outcomes. As you grow more self-reliant and capable with advancing language skills, you should understand that working together you can achieve more than what you may be able to by yourself.

Back to the essence of this book, from communicating in a foreign language to survive, to building meaningful relationships to thrive, the habit of delegating is powerful and widely applied. The art of delegation goes hand in hand with interdependence which relies upon the cooperation with others to get what you want and, crucially, help others get what they want. The more people you know and the more you know them, the better-informed and more empowered you can become in delegating. It's who you know!

CHAPTER 5

YOU CAN NEVER COMMUNICATE IN ONE LANGUAGE

"If you talk to a man in a language he understands, that goes to his head. If you talk to him in his own language, that goes to his heart." — *Nelson Mandela*

I expected you to have started this chapter with question marks around the idea in its title. An expanded version of this key philosophy goes this way: you do not necessarily need to speak more than one foreign language to be a Multilingual Connector but you always need more than one language to communicate and connect with anyone, including those who speak your native language. Even though you may identify as monolingual or bilingual, you should already be applying more than one language to communicate and connect in your day-to-day life – to make you wonder more.

DAISY WU

EVERY CONNECTOR IS MULTILINGUAL

By common definition, we usually identify someone as multilingual if that person is able to use more than two languages for communication. Given this, at first sight, the identity of a Multilingual Connector may not appear relatable to you as you have only learned one language apart from your mother tongue and therefore you would rather describe yourself as bilingual instead of multilingual as per the common notion.

Let me illustrate my point first with the definition of the word 'language'. In both the Collins and Cambridge dictionary, it is defined as a system of communication comprising sounds and written symbols. More than likely, you will interpret this as a reference to one or a cluster of languages amongst the over 7000 languages spoken across the world today. Yet bear in mind, being able to speak and/or write in a structured and logical way is not the only way to convey meanings to other people. For certain populations with special needs, they use sign language with visual-manual modality to convey meaning, or Braille, a tactile reading and writing system. Such terms as body language and visual language should also not be foreign to you. Notably, be it language as an umbrella term or collective terms like the aforementioned other forms of language, language is commonly referred to as *a* system of communication, not 'the' system. Note the article in its definition is non-specific. This suggests that what most of us define as the dominant means of communication is at best one of the important subsets of the entire system of human-to-human communication. The languages we read, listen, speak and write are by no means the only system for communication.

MULTILINGUAL CONNECTORS

You may have experienced it personally or know somebody who has travelled or even lived overseas without speaking local languages well or at all. With limited access to a translator or dictionary, it is still possible to communicate with the local residents via body gestures, facial expressions, hand sketches or any other creative means you resort to.

When illustrating my Multilingual Connectors Framework at the beginning, I briefly explained the general categories of communication, namely verbal (oral) communication, written communication and non-verbal communication. Non-verbal communication is the collective term for body language and facial language. It refers to the act of conveying information without the use of words that also encompasses the use of voice, touch, social cues, objects, kinesics, distance and physical environments as well as appearance. In line with the main message of this book, building intercultural connections without language mastery, the word 'multilingual' in Multilingual Connectors depicts language as semantic (relating to the meanings in words or logic). In reference to the MLC Framework, languages can also be emotional, psychological, cultural and situational. The energy exchange between two individuals communicating is both multidimensional and multisensory. Having a good handle on non-verbal communication tools is an indispensable quality of Multilingual Connectors who can build a strong and diverse network without over-relying on the languages they speak and write.

COMMUNICATION GOES BEYOND WORDS

Speaking confidently remains a conundrum that plagues many

foreign language speakers. Despite the broad literature supporting the importance of non-verbal communication, it is not very easy to outgrow the feeling of needing to word things correctly. Feeling anxious and as though we are deficient can still haunt us every so often, as we worry about getting the words spot-on. This phenomenon still exists within advanced language learners, whether in speaking and writing.

A frequently cited study by Albert Mehrabian, UCLA's Professor Emeritus of Psychology, says that when you communicate your feelings and attitudes, your actual words only convey 7% of the message whereas your body language and tone of voice represents 55% and 38% respectively. A common misinterpretation of Mehrabian's findings is that over 90% of communication is non-verbal, creating the illusion that non-verbal signals are far more important than words. To debunk Mehrabian's formula, simply remember that while the non-verbal plays a role in communication, it does not dominate our communication or outweigh the value of words. To put Mehrabian's findings in this study into context, in situations where words and non-verbal messages are contradictory to one another, people are more likely to believe the non-verbal cues they see over the verbal cues they hear.

We all know how important first impressions are. The 7/11 rule illustrates this: on average people will form 11 impressions of you within the initial 7 seconds of meeting, assessing whether you're likable, competent and trustworthy. First impressions are more heavily influenced by nonverbal cues than verbal cues. A 2011 Forbes article cited studies to show that nonverbal cues are over four times more impactful in the impression you give someone than what you say. Given this and the above, it pays dividends to advance your understanding and command of non-verbal languages as they can complement the imperfections in your words and do you better justice where words fall short. I will introduce a few strategies for you to practice this principle.

The visual effect

In the abovementioned 7/11 rule, the 11 common impression people form about you within the first 7 seconds of meeting are your:
- Ethnic Background
- Education Level
- Economic Level
- Level of Sophistication
- Level of Success
- Orientation
- Perceived Credibility, Believability, Competence and Honesty
- Political Background
- Religious Background
- Social/Professional Desirability
- Trustworthiness

It is obvious from the above that people form most of their initial impressions based on what they see from you. Correspondingly, studies have shown that as human beings, we are wired in a way that we remember less than 10% of what we hear, 20% of what we read and 80% of what we see. Evidently, we are living in a world where people often judge a book by its cover. People today are becoming more visual than ever so you must learn how to connect with others visually.

When it comes to your physical appearance, I cannot re-emphasise enough the role of self-image. How you present yourself to the outside world is the exact projection of the person in the mirror of your own mind. Dressing decently and appropriately not only shows respect to the people you interact with but first and foremost, the due regard to yourself as the most important stakeholder in all connections. This does not mean you must wear luxurious or trendy clothing and accessories. As a starting point, your attire and presentation should be suitable for the occasion and live up to your self-image. Looking neat and presentable is a hygiene factor. Whenever the dress code is ambiguous, it is usually better to overdress a little than be underdressed, especially in professional or semi-casual settings. It helps to scan the room and do some background research to help you dress smarter in future.

Since what you are attired in can convey a strong message on who you are, I would just remind you of the danger of compromising individuality when referencing others on personal styles. As an example, the 'Casual Friday' dress code common in western offices is not something I subscribe to personally. In fact, this dress code exists to allow workers to express themselves and feel comfortable, which is subject to individuals' interpretations and preferences. I remain in my element without feeling constrained when I wear structured and conservative clothing such as shirts and blazers and would not really feel I'm serving myself right working in t-shirts and sneakers even for one day each week. For as long as you appear in front of others, even virtually, without talking, your outlook and presentation are constantly

MULTILINGUAL CONNECTORS

communicating in silence to educate others about you. I have attended and spearheaded many panel events and corporate functions where prospective young candidates join informational interviews and presentations at the host organizations they may apply for. I was startled at the sight of hoodies and jeans among some of the attendees in almost all instances and unsurprised to find out these people walking their talks in what they wear – typically, they do not conduct themselves as a future employee when networking, and display diminished confidence levels with a tendency of talking themselves out of the opportunity even before the company representatives form their own judgements.

Equally important as your attire are your gestures and facial expressions. Here are my recommendations for connecting better at a visual level with improved body languages:

1. **Smile:** It is a sign of welcome and an invitation. Do not just smile when greeting. Keeping a friendly and welcoming smile when you are speaking and listening throughout the meeting, this can enhance your rapport. According to Andy Andrew, New York Times best-selling author, less than 1 in 10 people naturally smile while they talk. This is an acquirable skill, not a talent. A simple tip is to practice in front of a mirror or record yourself for 90 seconds regularly till you can smile while you talk more effortlessly without feeling phony.
2. **Make lasting eye contact:** As you look at a person's eyes, it signals your openness and interest and imminently transmits bonding energy. The dodging or wandering eyes will disconnect.
3. **Have firm handshakes:** This is the most effective and fastest

way to build rapport. It has been found by research that it typically takes about 3 hours of continuing interaction to nurture the same level of rapport you can establish with one handshake. Step out with the foot on the opposite side of the hand you reach out to shake – at the same time. Do not forget to maintain eye contact when shaking hands.
4. **Lean forward slightly:** Leaning in indicates you are interested, present and engaged.
5. **Position your body upright and steady:** Straightening your posture helps to non-verbally convey confidence and competence. In fact, height and space speak volumes about status and power. Do not hunch over or keep your chin down. Avoid moving your body or adjust postures more frequently than the situation requires.

You can't go far with just your words

> *"It is your attitude rather than your aptitude that determines your altitude."* — Zig Ziglar

Exactly as the late Zig Ziglar once said, your attitude often overpowers the words you use.

Attitude is the super power that will either let people gravitate towards you or alienate them from you. It is not something that people see or hear from you, rather it is what you make them feel in presence or spirit. Therefore, on your self-improvement journey, you must place due regard to developing your personality to include an attractive attitude and optimal mental state. Your attitude, which relates to the way you perceive the world

MULTILINGUAL CONNECTORS

and yourself will precipitate your demeanour and behaviours and ultimately how others experience you, as illuminated before. Being a well-spoken messenger does not guarantee connection because people experience and interpret your attitude at the same time as your message with the former usually a dominant determinant.

I also firmly believe that attitude is also perceivable in written words. I keep this in mind throughout my book writing journey. To give a glance, there were countless times where I stagnated between sentences and paragraphs and regurgitated words and expressions. Even in the process of penning this section to argue around the role of the quality of our words, I was continuously and consciously battling with the obsession about perfecting the sentences. There was also some temptation to emulate the language from the literature where I sourced ideas, framework and research data. In most cases, this put me into analysis paralysis as I overthought the writing and underestimated myself. Eventually it is my heart that made the call to let the words flow out down onto the paper after sifting them through the brain and intellect. These were the exact words that first popped up in my heart when I recalled and entertained my sentiments towards the life experiences and philosophy I shared with the other Multilingual Connectors in my tribe.

Writing from the heart, not just the brain, is vital to writing well in a way that connects people with your attitude. Of course, it matters to be grammatically and logically sound and accurate in your word choice in specific settings. Even so, always remember the immense power of our attitude. Write in a way that is as if you are speaking to the reader as though they are right in front of you with honest emotion, open attitude and raw humanity.

With the rise of artificial intelligence (AI), some experts have begun to question whether AI will replace writers in the future. The past decade has also witnessed the emergence of AI-enabled virtual servants to perform customer service. While the advent in technology has made AI writers more powerful, AI has not advanced to a stage where it is capable of doing all of what human beings can. In respect to human-to-human connection, it is in essence the transfer of energy through emotions. While AI can recognize patterns, it does not have emotions like human beings which renders it generally viable to replace mundane, repetitive and robotic tasks which do not require creative thinking and emotional intelligence. Technology cannot replace the thinking aspect of connecting which relies heavily on interpreting people's emotional needs and wants as well as the nuanced thoughts. AI-generated content might be functional in some contexts, but in situations where you need to win people over and connect to their feelings, only we human beings can create the missing piece – with an attitude of gratitude and servitude paired with our critical and creative minds!

LANGUAGE SHOULD NOT BE A BARRIER TO GENUINE LISTENING

You may believe one of the key reasons for miscommunication is a poor ability to understand what the other person has said in your non-native language, and possibly your inability to get your point across precisely in your reply within the limitations of your vocabulary. Yet have you had such experiences where you believe

MULTILINGUAL CONNECTORS

you have comprehended every word said and smoothly, expressed what you want to say, but you and/or your conversation partner still struggle to understand each other?

Research shows we spend about 44% of our time listening, but it's rare for someone to be truly heard. Amongst ample literature on the importance of listening in communication, in the book *The 7 Habits of Highly Effective People*, Stephen R. Covey introduces the importance of empathic communication which is conditional on effective listening.

> *"If I were to summarize in one sentence the single most important principle I have learned in the field of interpersonal relations, it would be this: Seek first to understand, then to be understood."* — Dr. Stephen R. Covey

You probably believe you more or less live up to Stephen's key advice in that book chapter particularly in a foreign language. When listening to someone speaking in your non-native tongue, it is natural to focus heavily on translation to extract the literal meaning of what is being said. This is typically the bottom line when you are not very proficient in a language. As you advance in that language, at certain points listening may still be a challenge sometimes as the speed of speech, accent and density of language varies from one person to another. You are likely to devote a lot more attention to listening in your foreign language, especially in one-on-one conversations, for it would be very awkward for you to lose track – which may force the conversation to an end. You have possibly also endured moments when you are lost from the beginning or halfway in the dialogue but have to pretend you are still with the person talking. Like many of you would have, I have practiced my English listening through various means, and feel very rewarded when hard work pays off when my dictation and comprehension improves to match the subtitles of the movies I watch to practise – which also translates into better communication experience in real life. At one point, I believed my listening was actually better in a foreign language and didn't see any major aspect of it I needed to catch up on.

The real issue Stephen tries to address is that most people listen with the intent to reply, not to understand. Foreign language communication is not an exception whereby people want to make their points and be understood as the ultimate objective. Simply, after the translation as an additional process to communicating in one's native language, people still filter the information they gathered through their own life experience, beliefs and other frames of reference. With a pre-established agenda, they may be selective in their listening and pay attention to the information they believe is important for them to know. From there, they decide prematurely what the other person means before they finish talking. Poor listeners are either speaking or preparing to speak and do not seek first to truly understand what people are saying *and feeling* when in conversation.

Seeking to understand before being understood seems easy enough to do, but for many, it can be a difficult habit to develop. While language abilities can to some extent hinder one's comprehension which preoccupies some people, it should not be a barrier to genuine listening where you place the other person's emotions at the centre of your heart. Fundamentally, effective listening is a behavioural pattern, not a competency based on your level of mastery in a language. As will be explained next, it can be consciously cultivated and improved.

Key elements to effective listening in any language

> *Listening is "an **active process** which constructs meaning from **verbal** and **nonverbal messages**".*

– Active Process:

In contrast to passive listening, when one listens with limited or no response or feedback, actively listening involves acknowledging the speaker to show that you have heard them. When the other person feels they are being attended to and understood, he/she will be more likely to open their mind, creating fewer roadblocks in the communication.

As the differentiating factor between passive and active listening, the act of acknowledgement is highly crucial for non-native speakers. It goes one step beyond ticking the box of your understanding in your own mind – but also the other persons. Here are the two simple steps:

1. **Work on your mindset and attitude** by first recognizing the full benefits; it should not only help you understand but also make the other person feel understood! Listen with the genuine intention to make this the doorway to mutual understanding. Not only does it mitigate the risk of miscomprehension for you in a foreign language, but the action demonstrates your commitment to understanding the other person and overcoming the potential comprehension

challenges. When you make others feel heard through active listening, they will be more attentive and receptive to what you say in return.
2. **Check your understanding** by paraphrasing either in your own words or the exact terms they said. 'If I understood you correctly, (you were saying) … ', 'What I think I heard you say was … ' You must acknowledge the possibility that you may have misunderstood or made incorrect assumptions, and give others the permission to correct you. 'Please correct me if I didn't understand you correctly,' will do.

– **Verbal messages:**

In truth, all listening is selective. However, if you're too caught up with your own agenda and thoughts, you may risk missing out on some critical information in the other person's words. Even if you have a vast vocabulary and plenty of competent listening skills in any language, you could still easily disengage and disconnect in the conversation.

Empty your headspace before any form of interaction starts. We can get caught up in our own thoughts, ego, bias and judgement before those of the other person become transparent in their expressions. You are not actively listening if you are lost and preoccupied in your own thoughts. Somewhere in the conversation, if not at the very start, we tend to think we can predict what the other person is going to say, and therefore, our minds wander. When your mind filled up with things in your internal world it is just like a full cup on the brink of overflowing; once others' thoughts are poured in, it will brim out and not much will be retained in the cup.

– Non-verbal messages:

What is not being said can convey more than what is said. From facial expressions, body movement and posture to voice and tonality, you need to command various senses other than hearing to gather a blend of non-verbal signals including but not limited to the person's body language, facial cues, personality and character.

Find the right time and place and set expectations

To listen well, you must give your undivided attention and free yourself from as many distractions as possible. Studies show the human brain does not perform well while multitasking so you should not be listening to someone on any important matter when you are in the middle of other tasks. If the subject matter is highly crucial, it is also critical that the surrounding offers enough privacy and minimises the distractions from others. When you are intentional about picking the appropriate venue to have a conversation, the other person will feel you care about the subject matter and care about them.

Another key aspect of being an excellent listener is setting people's expectations early. If you are unable to listen and respond to the other person, consider how you would reply in a way that would acknowledge them but set up a better time and place. You should first acknowledge the importance of the message, and also tell the other person that you are not in a position to listen actively and attentively at that moment. You should invite the other person to meet at another time and even better, propose and find a suitable time and place for you both in the same breath. This is to assure the other person you want to listen to them when you are able.

If you are not highly confident about your listening skills in a language, you must take full responsibility for ensuring the setting is optimised to brace your listening. Remember, it is not just for your own benefit.

CROSSING THE BOUNDARIES

Do you ever feel you can communicate with others in your non-native language but you still have difficulties in getting along with other people, typically those outside of your own culture? In today's increasingly diverse workplace and interconnected world, we have expanding opportunities to interact and collaborate across national borders and cultural boundaries which also come with mounting challenges. In a Harvard Business Review article titled 'How Non-native Speakers Can Crack the Glass Ceiling', the research suggests it often isn't the non-native speakers' functional language abilities that hold them back. Rather, it is the decision makers' negative perception of their interpersonal skills and communication styles rooted in the cultural differences. At the backdrop of globalisation, cultural intelligence (CQ) is fast emerging as a desirable attribute in the 21st century workplace which is becoming increasingly culturally diverse. In the Cambridge dictionary, culture is defined as 'the way of life, especially the general customs and beliefs, of a particular group of people at a particular time.' Cultural intelligence measures one's ability to relate to and effectively work with people coming from different backgrounds and life experiences. As such, it is

MULTILINGUAL CONNECTORS

a defining quality of a Multilingual Connector who is not only aware of culturally diverse situations but also highly able to relate, and where relevant, adapt to people of distinct nationalities, races, religions, ages, genders, political beliefs, socioeconomic statuses, occupations and so forth. According to a Forbes article, some experts identify cultural intelligence as a great predictor of success in the connected world today.

The good news is, CQ is measurable, cultivable and improvable. The following 4 key capabilities for CQ are introduced by the Cultural Intelligence Center:

1. CQ Drive: nurture interest, curiosity, confidence and motivation during multicultural interactions.
2. CQ Knowledge: cultivate understanding of the types of similarities and differences between cultures without leaning into stereotyping certain cultures.
3. CQ Strategy: grow your awareness and capability to plan cross cultural interactions effectively in light of cultural differences.
4. CQ Action: develop the ability to adapt behaviours when relating and working with other cultures if the situation demands it.

The initial step towards developing your CQ is to understand your cultural values (CV). A concept closely associated with cultural intelligence, cultural values indicate people's preferences in the way they interact, communicate, plan and complete tasks. These preferences are neither superior nor inferior to one another, rather they simply portray preferences people have for how they navigate life. You can assess your own cultural values on the web page of Cultural Intelligence Center (https://culturalq

.com/products-services/assessments/cultural-values-profile/). The feedback report maps your preference in 10 cultural value dimensions. Included in the report is the Cultural Value Profiles of the world's 10 largest cultural clusters stemming from Ronen & Shenkar's research. This provides a starting point for benchmarking yourself against the dominant profiles of these clusters (e.g. Anglos v.s. Confusion Asians).

Knowing your own cultural preferences and how they compare with typical norms from other groups provides valuable insights that can help you understand other people's actions to become more culturally intelligent. Note the Culture Value Profiles are not to generalize or definitively predict the behavioural traits from anyone who you can identify from a cultural cluster. Rather, it is useful to apply the 10 cultural value dimensions as a matrix to dissect and better understand any peculiarity or idiosyncrasy you can observe from an individual.

Provided the common definitions and possibly your own experiences, you should also recognize that it is not just the national or ethnic boundaries that form cultural differences. Perhaps you're familiar with the term 'company or organization culture' and 'cultural fit' being a recruitment benchmark to cherry-pick candidates who share similar traits and aligned backgrounds as current employees. Within many organisations, there can also be subcultures within different departments and teams. When you join a new company or team, you typically spend the first few weeks navigating its cultural codes and norms, which is vital for you to perform your role on the job and importantly, find your feet in the new environment. Whether in professional or social settings, within or beyond your one cultural-ethnic

MULTILINGUAL CONNECTORS

group, being culturally competent will enable you to integrate well in an environment and thrive interpersonally.

In addition to the abovementioned Cultural Value Profile, there are other tests which can improve your grasp of your psychological profile and other people's to have fruitful communications. For example, the MBTI Personality Test based on Isabel Briggs Myers' and Carl Jung's personality type theory is the most widely used and recognized personality tool to illustrate the 16 dominant archetypes. More recently, in the book of Victor Gulenko published in 2019, he identifies 64 personality portraits in socionics. Gulenko's work was cited on the podcast of author and motivational speaker Jay Shetty, where Shetty simplified the 64 personality types into four. These four quotients are formulated by whether a person is more outgoing (for the letter 'O') versus reserved ('R') and more people-focused ('P') and task-oriented ('T'). You could identify one letter for each personality trait in reference to how you typically behave in social situations. The combinations of these letters form the 4 types: OP, RP, OT and RT. I personally enjoy that episode and highly encourage you to explore your personality type and learn some techniques to grow more interpersonally effective in your interaction with the 4 types you will meet in life in Shetty's *On Purpose* podcast.

Looking beyond those traits, here is a list of simple and practical steps for you to advance your cultural intelligence and interpersonal effectiveness:

1. Once in every while, have interesting and eye-opening conversations with people from a background with experiences and beliefs which are very different from yours.

2. Develop an open mind and active listening skills. This ties to CQ Drive as the first capability required for cultural intelligence discussed above. Having the inner drive and curiosity to understand other people is a pivotal starting point.
3. Reflect on the biases that can narrow your vision. It's important to identify the sources of these biases that could be rooted in your own cultural heritage and upbringing which influence your worldview. Likewise, find the sources for the biases that may exist in your organisation.
4. Consume content from across the globe to widen your worldview and appreciate how other cultures view the world. Where practical, immerse yourself in cultures and perspectives other than those you are familiar with. Travelling is a tremendous way to do this. Alternatively, attend events, any type where you anticipate a group of people with distinct backgrounds.
5. Read and watch content which demonstrates opposing opinions and perspectives in the mindset of seeking to understand what is valued by those at the other end of the spectrum. This is conducive to improve your nuanced thinking skills instead of always thinking in binary terms.

CHAPTER 6

'NON-NATIVE ENGLISH' IS OUR SUPERPOWER

"Locate your weakness because the strongman takes advantage of it." — Dr. D. K. Olukoya

There is vast research which suggests that speakers of multiple languages have advantages in work and in life. However, many bilingual and multilingual speakers are not intimately aware of their advantages and usually pay more attention to overcoming their shortcomings and imperfections in a foreign language. Quite often, where the dominant language is not their mother tongue, many tend to focus on how they may be disadvantaged as a non-native speaker. With 2 billion non-native speakers dominating the English-speaking world, there exists a multi-billion English-as-a-foreign-language industry which trains people to speak decent and authentic English. Just try Googling 'how to speak English like a native,' and see how many search results pop up.

As a non-native English speaker who's come to terms with the foreign language communication style she was once desperate to outgrow and turned her limits into strengths, I want to dedicate this chapter as an antidote to the never-ending qualm about not being native-like enough in your non-native language. Like many of you, I couldn't see the end of the tunnel to master authentic 'Aussie' English when I just moved to Australia. However, my collective experience in one of the most culturally and linguistically diverse western countries led me to the revelations I wish I'd known as early as possible: 'non-native English' is our superpower.

It's not enough to just know where the superpower comes from in our respective background but how we can lean on our unparalleled advantages over the monolinguals or native (English) speakers to thrive interpersonally in intercultural settings. Whether you think you are incompetent in a foreign language or relatively proficient but not native-like enough which puts you at a disadvantage, this chapter is not to be missed.

WHAT ACTUALLY MAKES YOU FEEL BAD ABOUT YOUR DECENT ENGLISH?

There is no better example than accents to illustrate what lies at the root of the widespread qualm about not being or resembling the native speakers, given a widespread compulsion for correcting accents to mimic those from the UK and Commonwealth countries where people speak 'mainstream' native English. Many

MULTILINGUAL CONNECTORS

people still feel inadequate and inferior in their non-native language due to a thick foreign accent, even when they already have near native proficiency in the language. From a linguistic point of view, an accent is a distinctive way of pronouncing a language which can typically identify its speakers in a particular country, area, or social class. Everyone has an accent so a 'correct' or 'standard' accent in the common notion does not practically exist.

Despite the objective facts, accent bias remains widely seen. In a recent study conducted by the Sutton Trust, almost 50% of employees in Britain have been criticised and marginalised due to their accent. Although there is yet to be widespread research evidence on how accent impacts the perception of the speaker's characteristics such as intelligence, physical attractiveness, trustworthiness and social prestige, the impetus for such studies over decades has made the unconscious and conscious bias around non-standard-accented speakers tangible.

A key driver of accent bias is a self-constructed social identity. While accents may identify the locality in which its speakers reside and potentially their ethnicity and socio-economic status, an accent by its own nature does not objectively make one superior or inferior to the individuals from other social groups distinguished by their accent. Even so, many people have concerns about the bias and discrimination due to their accents. In the abovementioned study by the Sutton Trust, 23% of people are self-conscious about their accent and 19% have concerns over the negative impacts of their accent on their career prospects. For me, more profoundly, behind the accent and the way I spoke my non-native language was an array of facts about myself I'd wish to hide: that I didn't really belong in this foreign country, that

I was quite fresh here as predictable from both my fluency and accent, and that I was not well established in any profession or industry from my limited command of jargons and terminology – which boiled down to this inner voice 'I am not good enough especially due to my English skills, to deserve your attention, care and support … '

At its root, accent bias is actually under the guise of an under-developed self image that ramifies such feelings of insecurity and inferiority. Simply put, you can feel inferior due to many factors other than your accent and language proficiency, with or without external influences. Unless you develop an expansive self concept and mental toughness, you can still feel undeserving and unconfident with a constant sense of scarcity even when you are actually above average in many aspects. The points of comparison are endless. This emphasises the notion that the person who has got the greatest influence over the quality of your connection is in fact yourself, because you can hardly outperform your self-image.

With the above mentality, it is also common to see people, myself once included, endeavouring towards a beautiful accent in an attempt to favourably impress others. Though such behaviour is understandable and relatable, an accent by its own nature is not sufficient enough to create long-lasting desirable impressions, as also holds true for high fluency and a good command of vocabulary. In the bigger picture, where the focus is ultimately connecting with people, your accent does not matter as much as your words, which are just as important as the other non-verbal communication elements as discussed in the chapter before.

MULTILINGUAL CONNECTORS

OVERTURN THE STEREOTYPES IN YOUR FAVOUR

Moreover, if you remain a dedicated member of the 'native-like English club' and are conscious of common stereotypes, quite likely you haven't thought about the possibility of leveraging your natural communication style to create an even better impression than if you delivered it in a 'better' accent in your target language. In other words, what you may wish to eliminate is your unique asset which can help you create lasting and positive impressions with people, especially the native speakers in the target language. How is this possible? I would boil the secret sauce down to the 'expectation gap' which I will reveal in my experience below.

From attending the first professional networking session to teaching the first university class in Melbourne, quite often somebody will ask me where I am from shortly after I speak in English. Does that make me think my accent sabotages me? I used to think so, in the early days when I was very insecure and sensitive about giving away my secret – that I didn't really belong there (this was at a phase when my written English would nearly cover it all up till I opened my mouth). Even as I grew more fluent over time, when I spoke, I was self-conscious and concerned about my speaking style which I feared may bog me down. Similarly, it took quite some time for me to put into perspective such remarks as 'your English is quite good (as a Chinese person who's only lived here for a couple of years)'. I tended to interpret it with a self-deprecating outlook wherein I falsely assumed the other person meant nothing but sarcasm or was just giving impractical feel-good comments from a vantage point to tell me to take things easy while I was still stressing about not speaking good English. Instead of inviting them into my world and stepping out to make further contact, I would play out all the negative comments and attitudes in my head. This is precisely what made me talk less and less until a window would appear for us to exit the interaction, whilst trying my best to refine my accent waiting for the day when my self- and social image would improve along with it. In principle and practice, things never worked out this way.

It turns out that these people weren't usually asking such a question in an effort to offend or embarrass me. In many instances, the person enquiring was genuinely curious about how I'd established myself as a foreigner having come so far. While my English must not have sounded very native-like, there was a more than moderate likelihood that the other person was prepared to praise my English which had advanced within only a few years overseas. I was way too caught up in my own insecurity to leverage other's curiosity to connect with them.

Learning from my mistakes, I became more comfortably transparent about where I came from and leveraging the mental techniques introduced before, I shifted the focus to what the other person should care to know about me for their own interest and benefits. In front of my new students, I would tell them how I found myself in the same class years ago. 'I wasn't smarter than anyone back then and wasn't sure if I could survive the course fully taught in English. I'm more than happy to share how I made it in this subject and degree and believe you can definitely do it too.' My background as a former international student and non-native English speaker was actually a powerful bonding

MULTILINGUAL CONNECTORS

agent between me and the students in a culturally diverse cohort. Within the domestic students from whom I would typically get the enquiry about my nationality, I earnt their respect as I walked my talk to demonstrate the possibility of making good progress from almost 'ground zero'. With a new acquaintance or stranger who freshly discovered my origins, there was simply so much more for both of us to pay attention to in the moment than the fashion in which I spoke the language. Over time, I learnt to harness my identity as a foreigner as a key to unlock what I wanted to know about those who came on my path. In equal measure, I captured their curiosity about me before and after I lived in Australia within the limits of my vocabulary. Under such conditions, a good impression was simply the by-product of my high engagement and the presence, confidence and calmness I displayed.

Given the above, to leverage the expectation gap resulting from your natural accent does not translate to working harder to widen the gap between your actual language abilities and others' expectations based on perceptions and stereotypes. Indeed, the 'wow' effect does not stem from how well you command the language but essentially, how you carry yourself regardless of limited language skills. This not only affords you momentary attention during the initial contact but registers a positive image of you in the other person's mind.

Indeed, as a flag of our ethnic identity, our accent in a foreign language is so commonly underestimated as a point of disadvantage, which makes the notion of converting limitations into strengths sound far-fetched in this context. Let's put it into perspective, your accent is a sign of intelligence and diligence, because your hard work over months and years has paid off – you can now speak one more language than 40% of the world's population (who can only speak one language). Your accent is also a hallmark of vulnerability and bravery because you are showing up outside your comfort zone. Coupled with the right mindset to navigate conversations, your accent should enhance the perception about your dedication since you are speaking in that language – the person listening does not speak your native language at all (or as well as you do in *their* native language). Referencing my teaching and mentoring experience, it is only when you care a lot about others and their problems (that you may be able to solve) that you will exert yourself in a non-native language to lean in and speak up, instead of cringing and stepping back.

Whilst leaving you with the notion of your accent being your secret weapon, I want you to distinguish accent from pronunciation. Simply explained, pronunciation is the way a person pronounces each syllable of a word, which can be accurate or not. On the other hand, an accent is the distinctive regional variations of the same language in terms of rhythm and melody. In other words, while there is standard and correct pronunciation(s) in a language, it is not the case for accents. Accents are just like the way the same song sounds differently when played by different instruments. It is worth noting that accent is just one part of pronunciation – although arguably not the most critical part in comparison to clarity and accuracy which are more important for the ease of comprehension. As prior research indicates, people are more likely to believe things which are easier to process and understand and correspondingly, they trust in information less when it is delivered in a foreign accent rather than a native accent. With the role of accent put into perspective, you should now know the right focus when working on your pronunciation: the goal is to be better understood, at both a literal and personal level.

SIMPLICITY IS BEAUTY

> *"The finest words in the world are only vain sounds if you can't understand them."* — Anatole France

Intuitively, people may assume the 2 billion non-native English speakers are largely responsible for the miscommunications with those from the 400 million who were born into the English language. Nevertheless, research over decades shows that understanding and effectiveness in communication go down when a native English speaker enters a conversation among non-native speakers. In light of prior research, it is not merely the judgement and bias from native English speakers to non-native speakers, whether actual or perceived, that impede communication. As global communication specialist Heather Hansen identified, communication difficulties also intensify because the native speaker doesn't know how to speak the way non-native speakers naturally do, namely in a fashion accessible to an average person using simple words and phrases. Often, a native speaker's unconscious use of esoteric idioms and unnecessarily confusing vocabulary makes language less accessible to someone who is not as proficient in that language.

Whilst such causes of communication difficulty should

resonate with many foreign language learners including myself, from our end, the endeavour hardly ceases towards advancing language proficiency with diversified and refined vocabulary and grammar. When I read books and news articles and watched people talking in TV dramas and movies in English at a young age, I would dream about being as proficient as the authors and actors. After moving to Australia, I felt initially overwhelmed by the real-life conversations with native speakers as they were hard to comprehend sometimes. From day one, I set the goal of improving my English to be more authentic and native-like. In the first few years, I was obsessed with applying as many new words and phrases as possible to memorise better. I had a strong belief that people would be well impressed by the use of advanced phrases and grammar. Over nearly a decade of endeavour to turn words into possibilities in my second language, I have admittedly been from time to time guilty of overcomplicating the language. Though it can be tricky to tell the sophisticated vocabulary from the rest of the new vocabulary to pick up, a long period of immersion in the target language should provide you with more context to refine your communication.

Given the research insights, we should appreciate the nuances in the notion that being an advanced language user does not necessarily qualify someone as an effective communicator let alone a Multilingual Connector. If the ultimate goal is to communicate as effectively as possible for the ease of building connection, it is counterproductive to overwhelm and overpower the recipient of your message with big and complex words and phrases. However, people with different language proficiencies are found to engage in such behaviour consciously and unconsciously in

MULTILINGUAL CONNECTORS

various settings. While the mastery of a foreign language could be a partial indicator of your intelligence and education level, the language should be a medium to make information and insights as cognitively accessible as possible and therefore making your character, knowledge and competence tangible to the other person. With this being the main focus in communication, you should worry less about the scarce use of advanced vocabulary, phrases and jargon when speaking or writing in a foreign language. Even though it is important to pick them up as part of your receptive vocabulary or passive vocabulary to improve your comprehension, not all of them need to be your working vocabulary in real settings. It is also important to note that just because someone communicates to you in a complicated manner doesn't mean you must mimic their style in response especially if they already make themselves hard to comprehend. If you find a presentation confusing, eventually you will need to translate and distil the contents in the working language accessible to yourself and any others you need to relay the information to.

In light of the study results above, if you are nowhere close to native or bilingual proficiency in a language, chances are you are at a vantage point to practise and master the art of simplicity. In case you are not aware, the foreign language vocabulary and grammar you have mastered, however limited they appear to you, already give you a head start! As long as you are able to communicate with others and get things done, you are enough and in fact, you are brilliant! While you are striving to gradually enrich your vocabulary and refine your language, here is a guide for you to improve the use of simple language to get your point across in a decent and effective manner to facilitate better connection:

1. **Simplicity starts from clarity:**

    'Have an understanding so there won't be a misunderstanding.' To apply this, you must be able to paint a clear picture of the subject in your mind before you can say or write it clearly and concisely. Anytime people struggle to articulate an idea in a way easy to comprehend to an average person or layman, it's a sure sign that they don't possess a decent understanding of it. Begin with the end in mind. You have a clarity about the key objectives of communication which formulate your train of thought, whether you are writing or speaking, in a spontaneous setting or not. You should always have your listeners and readers in mind and consider what they need to know, which brings me to the next point.

2. **Know your audience:**

    As one of the common communication advice points, you must consider the level of proficiency of the people you communicate to in your target language. Stay observant of the way they write and speak that language to gauge and do your background research when needed before initial encounters. If you want to take your communication to the next level and connect effectively with people, your language won't serve you if you use too many words and phrases that are way more advanced than their level of comprehension in an attempt to demonstrate your competency and make a good impression. 'People don't care how much you know until they know how much you care.' To draw on Roosevelt's wisdom here, your care about the audience should translate to thoughtfulness in making communication between you easier as the first step towards nurturing connection.

MULTILINGUAL CONNECTORS

3. **Adapt to different situations:**

Knowing your audience also extends to understanding the context in which the communication takes place as the communication styles in terms of language use can also vary between settings. Note that simplifying and sharpening your language does not equal being casual and informal in certain settings. Also, in some situations it may not be the most appropriate to skimp on formal expression, terminology and jargon and extensively use plain language, defined by the U.S. government as 'communication your audience can understand the first time they read or hear it.' In general, you should pay attention to the accessible and suitable style of communication.

4. **Learn from the feedback**

Further to the point above, the feedback from those you've communicated with provides invaluable practical references for your continuous improvement. One way to extract feedback is by checking other people's understanding. You can pay attention to how they relay and paraphrase to check their understanding and respond to what you've said or written. Usually, the other person's paraphrase represents the most accessible version of the message to him or her which yours could've been simplified to. From there, you can refine your language to be clearer and simpler, which is more effective and efficient than using a dictionary and translators.

A big hurdle to forge connection is making yourself understandable, relatable and approachable to the other person. When it comes to your communication habits, the key quality is being accessible, not being advanced. For the English language, by virtue of being a member of the 2 billion people who acquired this foreign language in the classroom, you are already ahead of the game!

ADVANTAGES OF MULTILINGUAL CONNECTORS

There have been countless times when I wish I'd attended an international school in China with an immersive English environment or been born to an immigrant family in the western world. Such wishful thoughts would often strike me when I felt socially embarrassed or deficient due to language and cultural barriers. However, later, the twists and turns eventually led me to discovering the missing pieces of the puzzle to pivot my thinking and action. Instead of fixing my English to appear more native-like or extroverted to fit in, I retained and sharpened my immigrant's and introvert's edge which carved out my trajectory on the back of a strong multicultural network which accelerated my progress.

> *"A smooth sea never made a skilled sailor."* — Franklin D. Roosevelt

In retrospect, the ebbs and flows of living in a western country as a Chinese immigrant built me up as a whole individual which I wouldn't have got to experience had I settled for a predictable and perhaps more futureproof pathway in my hometown with relatives in close proximity. As destined to be, the endeavour towards language mastery set me on the path of self-mastery to navigate the interpersonal challenges accompanied by the language barrier

MULTILINGUAL CONNECTORS

once upon a time. From having zero knowledge about a new language in the classroom to having zero experience of using that language in an authentic foreign setting, every milestone is a beginning along the journey we are all privileged to embark on to learn one of the most common cross-border communications in the world: the sweat and tears behind learning from scratch and starting over and over, the embarrassment at mistakes, the ego hits upon rejections, the frustration over stagnation, the fear of lagging behind, the joy of breakthroughs, the sheer confusion, the fluctuation of confidence … All these big and small moments of learning and applying a language give us an additional layer of humility, empathy and tolerance towards others.

Understanding the working definition of 'multilingual' in 'Multilingual Connector', you should appreciate the privilege and advantages such an identity affords. Truly, in the process of advancing in English as a second language, I also upgraded my vulnerability, relatability, persistence, resilience, growth mindset and dedication to others. They are instrumental building blocks to construct my culturally diverse tribe which led to the birth of my thought leadership. A true embodiment of my advantages, I am closely connected to the experience and perspectives which formulated this book to empower and enlighten those experiencing the same fear, frustration and stagnation as I did so that they can break out of the mental prisons and no longer feel disadvantaged by their cultural and linguistic background.

I would like to conclude this chapter with an excerpt of my recent speech for TEDx Unimelb in a keynote, titled "Being A Non-native (English) Speaker Is An Advantage":

"Connection is something we should've all experienced but

not in all sorts of interactions, not simply when we use any language to get the point across and get things done in many of the superficial and functional communications in daily life.

For those of you still worrying about language skills, I want to tell you from experience:

Because I'm a non-native speaker, I cherish all interactions as a doorway to learn from the other person in a different language rather than just a stepping stone to drive personal agenda.

Because I'm a non-native speaker, I find it easier to be a good listener and stay curious and open-minded.

Because I'm a non-native speaker, I am more conscious of playing to the strengths in my overall skill set beyond the command of language.

Because I'm a non-native speaker, I hardly feel entitled or complacent but hold myself to earning respect through good causes of action to add value to others first.

Because I'm a non-native speaker, I am often reminded of how far I've come and that I should share my story more to inspire and re-educate more people.

That's why I'm here."

CHAPTER 7

DECODE THE KPIS OF YOUR 'KPI'S'

"Proximity is power." — Anthony Robbins

One of the more effective ways to fast-track your growth and development is to lean into the experience and insights of others. Though it is possible to be highly independent in the pursuit of your end goals, it will take an elongated period without access to the support and resources from others given the finite amount of our time and knowledge.

Do you find yourself lowering your standards and expectations just to 'fit in' and 'keep the peace'? Or, when you express your dreams and desires, do those around you tell you you're 'too ambitious' or do not know what to advise to help you reach the goals when they haven't achieved most of their own? Is there someone who believes in your potential and encourages you to try out new things and go for the opportunities you hardly dare to dream of? Your response to such questions indicates the way you are affected by the people in your surroundings.

You must understand the landscape of your connections that make up your inner circle and beyond in terms of the roles they play on your journey. Look at your connections in the context of what you have or wish to achieve in various domains in life, spiritual, relational, vocational, fiscal and personal. Do not forget that it is you who is the most influential person in deciding how you and the other person should connect meaningfully with each other.

Everyone has their own working definition for a connection vs a contact and is driven by varying objectives behind forming and maintaining connections at different life stages, which was explained before. Therefore, I am not going be highly descriptive about who you should connect with using any one-dimensional criteria, such as accountants, lawyers and doctors based on professional expertise, or family members and non-family members based on biological relationship, or confidants, friends, acquaintances and strangers based on level of intimacy. It is important to recognize though, that not all connections are the same and there is a degree of difference in how each of them influences your life. In this light, there are individuals who can be classified as your 'key people of influence' ('KPI's') on our trajectory and, on their own merits, the key performance indicators (KPIs) of our social network and life trajectory.

Appreciating this, in this chapter I will illuminate some overarching principles and philosophy to guide the formulation of your own rules to define your circle, that is, the KPIs of your 'KPI's'!

MULTILINGUAL CONNECTORS

YOU ARE THE AVERAGE OF ALL

The law of averages famously referenced by Jim Rohn should be familiar to you, whereby your results will mirror 'the average of the five people you spend the most time with' who embody our close circle. While appreciating the high influence of our close connections, I note his original statement relates to the law of averages – the theory that the result of any given situation will equal the average of all outcomes. Provided this and my own experience, I strongly believe that we are the average of all the connections that have crossed our paths, for such experiences have shaped who we are. Therefore, it is in your best interest to evaluate your connections in a broader circle, instead of only those closest to you.

To start with, ask yourself the following questions to identify a connection in your present and/or past:
- How long have you known that person for?
- What brought him/her into your life (and this intimately)?
- How have you both evolved since you first met?
- Have you become closer or more distant over time?
- What do/did you usually talk about?
- How does/did that person elevate your performance and thinking?

Following the above, to evaluate the outcomes of being associated with that person along the way, consider the questions below carefully:
1. **Are you playing big or small?**
We can feel small because we are living small. For those with low self-esteem and diminished confidence, it is very easy to get

into a rut and be conditioned to accept the status quo over time. You may start believing you cannot achieve anything better so cease trying, thereby creating a self-fulfilling prophecy without realising it. Recall from the other chapters that our interactions with the outside world can profoundly impact our beliefs and behaviour as they interplay with our self-image and confidence. It indicates that your social environment is very influential in shaping the scripts in your mind which dictate your behaviours and results.

I was once surrounded with international colleagues who struggled with language barriers and believed it was the top factor negatively impacting their career and life in Australia. Many felt it was more than normal to be outperformed by those speaking better English who may also have grown up in the local culture. Likewise, when I felt pigeonholed in my social network and worried I could not fare well in my university degree, my family and Chinese homestay echoed the belief that as Asian immigrants, we could at best find our feet on the sidelines of a western society and it would be good enough to land a corporate job after graduation.

Later, I was lucky to make new connections at volunteering ventures who had a more expansive mindset. Some of them proved the concept of becoming an asset in a multicultural society without advanced English skills. Working alongside them, I was propelled to diversify my extracurricular activities throughout my university curriculum which truly built me up. As my plate became fuller and I began dreaming bigger, some people would give well-intended advice such as taking things easy and prioritising self-care. Had I taken them at their word, I could not

MULTILINGUAL CONNECTORS

have probably achieved half of what I have in the same period of time.

Given mind mechanics being a common thread in multiple chapters, I cannot emphasise enough how easily you could become a by-product of the environment should you entertain the limiting beliefs of those within them. Whilst you may not always have 100% control over your external environment and the distance you keep from certain people, inside, you do have the full autonomy to accept or reject any idea that does not serve you well. In my family's case, I love and respect them but would not go to them first for personal development advice. Rather, I always benchmark myself against those who have achieved greater results in my areas of interest and inspire me to keep expanding.

2. **Are you pursuing new experiences?**

I highly appreciate my mentors for imparting the importance of a diversity of experience. Often, an underdeveloped self image and lack of confidence is caused by the lack of diverse experiences as you stay in your comfort zone with limited exposure to new circumstances and activities. This holds true for learning and using a foreign language, which lends itself to experiencing new things and meeting new people in a foreign environment.

When you traverse outside your routines and seek new experiences, you open yourself up to being challenged and inspired by new perspectives as you learn more about the world around you and yourself. You will seek solutions that you wouldn't have come up with any other way. Sometimes we can feel stuck in getting the same results that keep us where we are instead of propelling us where we want to be, after trying all the ways we could think of to find the way out. This is normal. No one knows everything.

We all have our own blind spots. There are things that we know we don't know, as well as those that we have yet to discover we don't know. In this light, the lack of diversity and breadth in our experiences can perpetuate our ignorance and stagnation. From time to time we need other people to point out our blind spots and unconducive behavioural and thinking patterns.

Moreover, as risk-taking is inherent in navigating new experiences, our network can also be instrumental in providing positive affirmations and emotional support. To be pragmatic, embracing risks does not amount to giving anything or anyone a shot in the confine of our time and resources. In this respect, my network encouraged and equipped me to take calculated risks. I could otherwise have remained in the survival or hibernation mode during the COVID-19 pandemic focusing only on finishing my master's degree and working in Melbourne. It is exactly the appetite for diverse experience and growth that kept me well connected in a more disconnected and isolated world when living alone. Despite the challenges during over 200 days of lockdowns, I relentlessly pursued new experiences that expanded me more than ever, including university tutoring, podcasting and mentoring. I cannot speak more highly of the influence of the growth-oriented and adventurous minds who live by example and inspire us to follow their footsteps and take the plunge.

3. **Are you growing or stagnating?**

An extension from the question above, I learnt from success educator and entrepreneur Ron Malhotra a simple way to measure growth is comparing the key problems occupying your mind between now and months ago. Suppose this time last year you were seeking a better job. Meanwhile, you could be stressed about speaking English confidently and finding the best avenue to network and improve in English. One year later, the key indicators of your growth may include tangible results, such as converting your dream job and becoming more socially confident in English. The more subtle yet critical measure I learnt from Ron is the quality of our thinking reflected in the questions you occupy your mind with, as translate to your understanding of your problems and your approach to resolve and/or outgrow them. To put it simply, if what was troubling or stressing you a year ago remains so, then you have not grown to either solve or leave your problems. This could be due to a few possible reasons: you may have not developed yourself to find the solution to the problems or change your outlook on the problems to let them dissolve that way.

An essential strategy to solve and leave your problems is to upgrade and advance them. Here is what the upgraded questions in the previous example may look like:

- How to quickly become a valued asset in your new workplace?
- How to be confident and effective in communications without native-like fluency?
- How to stay on top of minds without being the most talkative?

Otherwise, if the same questions still preoccupy you and have not been upgraded for you to pursue greater goals or optimise your strategies, it signals that your growth has been limited within the timeframe. Given the paragraphs above, it should be explanatory that the people around you can affect the quality of your thinking and in turn the results on your growth journey.

Based on the above meaningful questions, you can add more to suit your personal circumstances and evaluate your social surroundings. I'd suggest doing this reflection more often than simply once a year or when you feel in need of others' support and guidance, for it would then probably be too late for you to change. After the evaluation and reflection, you should be honest and open to the possibility that you may need to change your environment and who you spend the most time with and possibly seek new connections to better your growth and development. Do not feel guilty about drawing such conclusions.

THE CASE FOR COMPARISONS

Whenever I experience peer pressure, I am often advised to stop comparing myself with others. A common reminder that goes with such advice, is that it is critical to appreciate everyone is different and cut out for success in distinct forms. Notwithstanding this, as a natural human tendency, comparisons aren't inherently bad. One of its key functions is to form a baseline for where we are compared to others including those we admire, and where we want to be. Leveraged properly, it provides valuable information for self-improvement.

From my perspective, the results of the comparison are important, but arguably not as much as how you react to these results. It is 100% your call to take others' success and progress as a reminder of your inadequacy or source of inspiration. Likewise, you totally can control whether you derive lessons from others' failures and stagnation or entertain them as rationales for your inaction due to risk aversion or fear. Suppose you know a peer who makes many good connections from other cultures even without mastering English well, perhaps you feel inadequate and jealous, or maybe instead you could act upon your curiosity to bounce advice and feedback off that person to fast-track your progress and possibly develop a good friendship in doing so. If you already see yourself as being ahead of your peers, you can surely feel content and complacent about the status quo. Alternatively, you could also devote yourself to creating values to enable those who wish to get where you are and thereby hold yourself accountable for continuous improvement.

Comparisons can be a double-edged sword. They can be a powerful motivator, yet they sometimes also can be a strong deterrent to taking action with a positive perspective. It depends on how your mind interprets it.

So how do you avoid falling into the comparison trap and combat self-doubt? A key way to do this is to invest in yourself. It is important to work on yourself and set your mind to continuous improvement over lifelong learning so that you can reap the rewards and, in turn, help other people. This strengthens the case for having the people in your surroundings who possess the wisdom and knowledge to learn from.

THE 'KPI'S' FOR MULTILINGUAL CONNECTORS

With the above sections setting the tone, I will introduce three groups of key connections that embody some of the most critical functions integral to our growth and progress.

Peer

The Cambridge Dictionary defines a peer as 'a person of the same age, the same social position, or having the same abilities as other people in a group'. More generally, even if someone is not of similar age as you, so long as he or she is of equal standing with you in other regards (e.g. qualifications, background, social status), that person matches the working definition of a peer.

I could not conceive this book as an antidote to the widely quoted language barrier if I only had myself as the reference point. Until I met non-native English speakers from all over the world other than those from my home country, I could not start outgrowing the stigma around 'bad English' as a member of the population who in both stereotype and fact are on average not competent in speaking fluent English as a second language. When I joined a big firm, I was paired with a buddy. I now still thank her for ridding me of self-depreciating thoughts when I felt lost and yet expecting a lot from myself as a rookie. The peer support was invaluable from somebody who had started in my role with a Chinese-Asian background. A non-Asian senior manager would have also been helpful during onboarding but not from the exact same standpoint. The notion of not being the only person in this world experiencing the challenges I perceived is quite assuring and counteracts self-defeating thoughts.

This brings me to the second benefit of peer connection: actionable lessons that can often be derived from their highly relatable experience. Sometimes, when feeling stuck and lost, it is beneficial to look to those who have already achieved your next goal. You can use them as a reference to whether or not you're heading in the right direction, and potentially they can guide you

MULTILINGUAL CONNECTORS

towards the next best step. That person does not necessarily have to have reached your ultimate goal already, or be well ahead of you in that journey, but must have at least passed the next milestone you're striving to achieve. During my early career, I built a solid foundation of peer connection and compounded small lessons into incremental steps, from study tips, clubs and societies guides, time management advice to networking etiquettes and workplace transitioning.

The law of averages is highly applicable when you benchmark peer networks. One thing you should watch out for is herd mentality, namely the tendency of the people in a group to think and behave in ways that conform to those of the group to which they belong. Driven by the need to fit in and conform, people can be influenced by their peers to adopt beliefs and behaviours on a highly emotional as opposed to rational basis. When you are affected by herd mentality, you could make different decisions than you would have individually. Simply because many are doing and thinking in a certain way and it worked well for them does not mean it serves you the best. You should not blindly follow any practice without independent judgement.

Beware that peer influence may not always be conducive to your development and progress. Why? On their own merits, your peers are those with whom you share common ground and who generally are not substantially advanced from where you are. Typically, you turn to your peers for issues and matters in the short run, for example, work-related tasks. Even though you may find like-minded peers with aligned values and visions to share your long-term plans and goals, always keep in mind that by virtue of being your peers, they may not have much more diversity in the experience to learn the lessons and wisdom valuable to both of you. Although in this measure some of your peers may qualify to be your mentor, which I will explain next, within your peer network, there is a probable likelihood of the blind leading the blind.

Mentors

> *"A mentor is someone who sees more talent and ability within you, than you see in yourself, and helps bring it out of you."*
> *— Bob Proctor*

In the above quote, New York Times best-selling self-help author Bob Proctor well sums up the core benefits of mentoring. As you strive towards a better life in a foreign environment facing many unknowns, it would be a disservice to yourself forging ahead blind-folded without an outstanding mentor to help guide your way. Wouldn't you rather pick the brain of someone who has already reached where you aspire to be and learn what you would wish you had been told way earlier, instead of figuring it all out by yourself? In my understanding, mentors are in essence the ones whose hindsight can be leveraged as your foresight. Mentorship gives you the invaluable opportunity to stand on the shoulders of the giants. To see out your dreams, you need to invest in yourself in the relationships that nurture you towards where you want to go and would otherwise not have aspired for, but faster!

Speaking from experience, I strongly encourage you to look for additional mentorship beyond any institutions you are part

MULTILINGUAL CONNECTORS

of that have established mentoring structures. Whilst it may be convenient to connect to a mentor via the programs in your companies, industry associations and alike, the matching process may not be perfect and the capacity of mentoring is usually limited in duration and scope of involvement, which you do not have full control over. Wherever you see gaps in your life and find yourself stuck and lost, you surely should engage more than one mentor to help you develop more holistically. I have learnt from one of my best mentors to take 100% ownership over growth and development on my own terms. Mentorship is not an exception where you should always remain in the driver's seat along the journey. Down the track, you can have different mentors onboard to navigate the route to your next destination. In any event, mentors should remain in a position to guide and advise but allow you to preserve your full agency to follow their advice and guidance or not. Your mentors can influence your decisions but never overpower or override you by imposing their worldviews and ambitions. It is critical to remember at all times you are your own top person of influence and to know exactly what you want out of the connections you build. Otherwise, it would be too easy to wind up falling into other people's dreams and whims.

Appreciating how influential and instrumental mentoring relationships are, you should not loosely qualify anyone to be a mentor and then further so, your mentor. I would not be able to establish myself as an impactful thought leader at this point and write a book to spread my message if I had not ever invested in mentoring. Considering a mentoring relationship is a two-way street where you dedicate your time, energy and potentially money in exchange for someone else's guidance, you must do enough due diligence and cherry-pick your mentor. Simply because you believe you do not know much about something does not mean you should settle for anyone who might loosely qualify by appearing more experienced or senior. Here are a few considerations for selecting a mentor:

First and foremost, do you wish to become the person who your prospective mentor is? I am sure you would not entertain any networking advice from someone who is socially awkward. It is also possible that due to divergent interests, you are seldom inspired by someone's accomplishments regardless of how successful they are in that field. As simple as that, if you do not desire the life and results that person has achieved, then do not give them the right to mentor you.

Secondly, you should carefully assess the person's experience and expertise. Besides the subject-related expertise relating to the field where you have a problem to solve, mentoring is a standalone pivotal skill set. One may be highly skilled and knowledgeable but not as competent in imparting their knowledge and translating their solutions into actionable advice and steps for others to get results. You should therefore try your best to look for someone who has a track record of mentorship. The testimonials and word of mouth from their former mentees could be helpful. With a person's experience, apart from the relevance to your desired trajectory, you should not unconditionally equate many years of experience with broad and deep expertise. Though years of experience enables one to grow expertise, your due diligence should not stop at this superficial level. Recalling the importance of diversity in one's experience that I stressed earlier, you need to

MULTILINGUAL CONNECTORS

be cautious about picking someone who appears to have lived and worked abroad for two decades. There may not always be a decent mix of depth and breadth in the twenty years, which can effectively translate to one year repeated twenty times in the extreme case. For example, someone who has lived in the same country for five years may turn out to be a better mentor with a much more enriched trajectory with achievements more aligned with what you want.

Last but not least, do they walk their talk or just talk the talk? There are way too many people who pass on a solution randomly without any proof that it worked for themselves. Within this population, there is a high likelihood that they follow and/or pass on other advice without filtering the context and application. The person you choose to be your mentor must lead by example. He or she may not share the same or similar background or trajectory with you, though it would be ideal, but they must have overcome challenges of comparable if not greater magnitude using the exact philosophy to be imparted to you. In my own experience, I have been working with some of my mentors from establishing my early career in Australia to continuing my success in education and thought leadership. All of my mentors are native English speakers and the mentorship did not revolve about the book's core concept to solve the puzzle on whether the second language was to make or break me. Still, I applied and extrapolated their non-conventional insights on self leadership and success because I could see them applying these wisdoms and achieving exceptional results in multiple arenas. I owe them for the paradigm shifts at critical career pivots and on the path to becoming a thought leader.

DAISY WU

Allies and Advocates

"If you want to go fast, go alone, if you want to go far, go together." — African Proverb

Allies and advocates are also vital connections to accelerate your advancement. Having someone to vouch for and support you can make a positive difference when you feel under stress, unseen or unheard. They can be cultivated from your broader network, including but not limited to peers and mentors introduced above. You can build such connections in your workplace and other communities you belong to.

An advocate is someone willing to champion your cause and strive to improve how others perceive you. This person knows you well and appreciates what you contribute to the causes you may or may not be part of together. In a work setting, some people may mix up this idea with a mentor as sometimes they can find somebody who performs both functions. A key distinction is that an advocate not only supports but promotes you and actively looks for opportunities to advance your reputation and standing. A mentor assumes the responsibility of advising and guidance to support your advancement but will not generally be committed to campaigning and advocating on your behalf. An advocate does not necessarily have to be your mentor. In parallel, you should also grow allies who generally support you and are there for you when the need arises. Like advocates, they can be individuals or groups.

Please note that the categories explained above are neither

exhaustive nor mutually exclusive in that as you grow and evolve with your network, your roles to each other can also take on a new look over time. One day you could seek mentorship from a then peer of yours and become a peer mentor of someone else in the same period. There are vast opportunities of turning your peers, mentors and anyone else in your network into allies and advocates. In the remaining chapters, I will further introduce the why and how to develop allies and advocates who will have your back.

NOT ALL MEANINGFUL CONNECTIONS NEED TO BE LONG-LASTING

'The networking you've been doing all these years must pay dividends in years …' I would love to tell the exact person who said this to me: whatever you had shared with me today is already deeply appreciated, even if our paths do not cross again. It would be great to reap the seeds I plant over time, but not all causes of action need to be associated with a well-defined end or objective.

> *"People always come into your life for a reason, a season and a lifetime. When you figure out which it is, you know exactly what to do."* — Brian A. "Drew" Chalker

We often hear advice on playing long-term games and seed the relationships with good intentions. As eloquently embodied in Brian's poem, not every relationship can or needs to be long-lasting. Just like value can be created in the moment, over a period and a lifetime, they can either be lasting or momentary.

As an inevitable result of your growth and progression, you may find some of your connections evolving and/or stagnating whose values and lifestyles may not match your current version any longer. In that case, you do not have to cut them out completely but just keep the distance that serves both of you the best. If there is someone whose presence in your life is not conducive, you should look for ways to limit your time together and do not be afraid to switch the topic of conversation if things take a negative turn.

I often hear people describing networking as meaningless or superficial as they usually see such activities as a stepping stone to drive professional outcomes for themselves and have low motivation when they do not have any set agenda. What is often underrated is the value of a connection in the moment, which is not always attached to a transactional or functional objective. Instead, it is the opportunity to know that person in multiple dimensions and also make yourself known through the interactions. Even in a task-oriented or transactional setting, we are more than just our job titles. Hopefully this paragraph reminds you of the positive emotional experience of meeting someone where you thoroughly enjoyed your time even though your encounter did not result in a concrete outcome.

The changing dynamics of your relationships is a signal of your development and expansion, not a definitive and absolute reflection of your ability to keep the connections. While you come to terms with the fact that you have grown apart or distant, you should stay appreciative of where your paths crossed and how you hopefully benefited from each other. When deciding who you choose to be in your proximity, I draw a key lesson from my mentor Elinor Moshe: keep a distance from those who

MULTILINGUAL CONNECTORS

(only) want more *from* you and stay closer to those who want more *for* you.

NOT YOUR ASSET

The notion 'your network is your net worth' is frequently quoted to emphasise the importance of relationships in our lives and careers. True as it is, in my opinion the expression 'net worth' can make people think of dollar signs. Other terms such as 'social capital', 'social equity' and 'asset' also create similar associations. They all call to mind the issue of transactional relationships popularly associated with conventional networking. As suggested by the name, transactional relationships are pretty much all about transactions built around the primary focus of questions as such: What can you give me and what I am expected to give in exchange? Author and entrepreneur Jean Oel highlights in her book *Partnering* that our individualistic society has created a cult of self-interest, which impacts our ability to connect and relate meaningfully to foster collaborations and inspire innovations. Previously we addressed that connection is not all about you and your own interests cannot solely motivate others to bend towards you. Whilst building connections is a relevant subject in professional settings to fulfil functional objectives such as project collaboration, deals and job acquisitions, we can play to our own agenda, but we also need to make conversations more genuine and enjoyable to invoke deeper connection and trust fundamental to all transactions and desired actions. In simple practice, this translates into giving the other person the time and space to express themselves freely with the notion that you truly care about them and have the genuine intention to provide value.

The concept of matching or trading value in our network is also problematic. For one thing, value is by definition a subjective measure and cannot always translate in dollar signs. The value may not and does not have to reach equilibrium. Sometimes the act of kindness can be unconditional and does not need to be reciprocated. Furthermore, the underlying mentality of comparing value in the exchange pretty much translates into viewing others as a stepping stone to your goals who you may otherwise not bother to connect with.

What if you stop viewing the people you know and are yet to meet as a means to an end, but instead as the end itself – an authentic relationship with depth and meaning, be it personal or professional? When you genuinely see people as a gateway to deeper learning, an opportunity to be fulfilled in the act of giving and sharing, and a gift to be emotionally rewarded through nurturing friendship, your mindset will shift with your perceptions. What might have previously been viewed as a dollar sign, a referral or job offer becomes something much greater to invoke gratitude and fulfilment within you.

Feeling distant and disconnected from the other person is an inside job. How connected or disconnected you feel is determined by the meaning which you ascribe to that relation. Fundamentally, to what extent a connection is meaningful has very little to do with the other person, but yourself as the biggest influencer in your connections. Before starting to figure out how to build meaningful relationships, you need to know the all-too-important relationship with yourself, i.e. what do you

MULTILINGUAL CONNECTORS

value the most and what does meaningfulness actually mean to you?

CHAPTER 8

ALL ROADS LEAD TO ROME

"Chance favours the prepared mind." — Louis Pasteur

'One connection could change your life.' With a mountain of research and real-life stories supporting this notion, the compound effect of networking should resonate with many of you. Ideally, you would recognize that your own growth and progression only represents a fraction of the benefits: with at least two connections, there exists the potential of making a life-changing introduction and with even more connections, we can build a circle to amplify the compounding of successful connections. Acknowledging all these, it remains a key puzzle to solve, namely, where to cross paths with the connections with whom you could better each other's lives as we discussed in the previous chapter? As for the avenues to connect, if by default the word 'networking' makes you cringe, sweat or frown, for whatever reasons (your

MULTILINGUAL CONNECTORS

social confidence, language skills, personality traits, past experience, general perception about such activities or else), it makes every sense to be selective about the form of interaction if you truly care about connecting beyond business cards and pitches. As the most important stakeholder in your connections, you have the ultimate responsibility to ensure you move to and stay in situations which serve you right and propel you forward.

While it is objectively possible for connections to take root at any time and any place, most of us are still bound by geographic locations to a certain degree in the interconnected digital age and more critically, time, which is our most valuable asset. To conserve your precious time and other resources, you cannot act upon the literal meaning of 'anytime, anywhere' and count on luck and fortune, for it will totally subject you to external factors beyond your control as you surrender your own handle over what could happen in your favour. In the book *Get Lucky: How to Put Planned Serendipity to Work for You and Your Business,* co-authors Thor Muller and Lane Becker distil the eight key elements that set apart blind luck and planned serendipity. Literatures as such further support the possibility of fostering the conditions for connection to occur early and often.

As the chapter's title and opening quote imply, there are usually multiple pathways to reach your destination; nonetheless, by being intentional, strategic and prepared, you will stay on the ball to navigate the most effective routes and veer away from the detours and those that won't lead you anywhere. I will further introduce the principles and practises to equip you to plan and attract your luck as a Multilingual Connector!

BEFORE YOU GOOGLE FOR THE BEST PLACES TO NETWORK

Everyone is wired differently. It is normal to have a mix of personalities and profiles in the same room. It is also not uncommon to see connections forged within and across the barriers and boundaries that differentiate one social group from their counterparts. That said, it is important to note that whatever you feel about certain occasions is merely a reflection of your personal preference and historical experience and does not automatically translate as your competency and project your future performance. As emphasised before, connection is a learnable skill rather than a bestowed talent. I almost rated myself as socially incompetent when I felt like a fish out of water during pub drinks in my first years in Australia. However, it did not take a long time for the same people chit-chatting about sports and entertainment over beers and loud music to be impressed how it almost appeared second nature for me to stay in conversations during industry networking calmly and confidently, without being native speaking.

Referring to the means goals and end goals introduced in Chapter 2, you must begin with an end goal in mind. As the enabling step for preparation, the what and why must emerge in your headspace before the how's. Don't just be obsessed with the tangible and easily measurable results which often fall under the category of means goals, such as offers, deals, referrals or simply more names on your contact list. Focus more on the end goals which in this context are constructed from your desired feelings throughout the process of interacting with the other person. Do

MULTILINGUAL CONNECTORS

you wish to feel confident and calm? Do you seek to be well understood, heard and appreciated? Would you prefer to feel welcome to lead the conversations as much as you want? Would you want to feel trusted by others to share what you are curious to know about them? The very reason why I reintroduce this concept is because typically, the greater the focus is on emotions instead of transactions and on connecting instead of dealing, the less significant the venues and occasions to maximise the odds of connecting with the 'right ones' per your own definition.

I will elaborate the above perspective with reference to the concept of multiplexity in David Burkus's book, *Friend of Friend*. In Burkus's terms, each connection you have is either a uniplex tie or a multiplex tie. When you have a uniplex connection, you have a single context or reason to know or meet someone. For example, you may have uniplex ties with most of your workplace colleagues you interact with on work projects. With others, you may form a multiplex connection wherein there are various situations and contexts in which you are in touch and associated with each other, who can be some of your co-workers sharing hobbies and/or participating in the same volunteering program with you regularly. An important research finding revealed in Burkus's literature is that you build a deeper relation faster with people with whom you have multiple ties. The lesson is to establish common ground to accelerate initial rapport for further bonding. For the multiplexity tactic to work out, you should identify the domains to create value for each other and note that the reciprocity can take place in two different domains. That means, even if you are in front of a person of higher status in your field or from a completely different arena which makes it seemingly harder to identify similarities, you still have the opportunity to build a relationship. The key habit is to look at a person beyond your default first impression. Once you seek to know a person in totality, you can diversify the directions in which you establish shared interests and touch points. With the avenue to foster connections in the focus, it is true that the venue and occasion play a role in facilitating the uniplex tie and possibly the multiplex ties. Examples of this can be professional associations, conferences, alumni networking, public speaking functions, cultural events and volunteering ventures, all of which could be good platforms for relationship building. Even so, it ultimately falls upon you and the other person to navigate the domains to create value and exchange your energy.

In reference to the networking science of multiplexity, here is my advice to improve your chance of building the desired connections you hope for:

- Apply the rule of multiplexity to be more creative and strategic in the selection of networking avenues. Remember that you do not always need to meet at events or functions. Within your organisations, it is relevant to turn a 'meal pal' into a comrade and potentially confidant. If you know a co-worker from a different culture as a fan of your home country's cuisines, don't hesitate to send an invite to introduce that colleague to the most authentic local restaurant in your current city, especially if he or she is someone you've always wanted to know better and be closer with.
- Leverage the compound effect to build a raft of touch points and context to deepen your bonds with someone. In the example above, the bonding starts with your shared interest

MULTILINGUAL CONNECTORS

in cuisines, which may seem superficial and shallow on top of the working relationship. Nonetheless, it is up to you to navigate more common ground together down the track to accelerate and strengthen the bond.

- Demonstrate real interest to find out more about other people's likes, habits and hobbies so that there is a greater likelihood to connect with them outside of the main agenda and where there is a power imbalance. To do this, you can leverage the small talk following initial greetings and at the intervals of main topics.
- Challenge yourself to diversify the topics and activities in your interactions. This should not only span any ice-breaking talk but extend into deeper and more meaningful discussions around a person's dreams, goals, personal philosophy and critical experiences that define his or her trajectory. If you can't get too deep into this in the initial encounter, due to time constraints or you choosing to stay at arm's length and professional distance initially, you should keep it in mind to explore other ground to underpin the connection when you touch base and reconnect.
- Stay in touch and in tune with your network. As will be further introduced later, social media platforms can be a powerful and efficient means to keep abreast of your connections. When it is not viable to reconnect through a meet-up online or in-person, content sharing and messaging can enrich your understanding of each other and spark common interests as you get to know each other better over time.

'Good luck is the result of good planning.'

I will leave you with the above quote to conclude this section. Remember, how you entered each other's world initially does not always dictate where you will go from there onwards.

1-ON-1 IS NOT ALWAYS BETTER

Many people who do not love to socialise often associate networking events with a negative connotation. Formal or casual, some find it draining and often daunting to engage in small talk and agenda-driven conversations in a room full of strangers. Those not using their first language typically share the same sentiments, if not even stronger. It is not uncommon for people to prefer individual meet-ups over group events, especially the introverts. A one-on-one setting is often believed to have a greater premise to connect closer via more personal and intimate conversations in the absence of interruption from another person. Even though a person can feel more nervous on their own having a dialogue with another person, people generally gravitate towards one-on-one conversation as the stepping stone to deeper connections. If you still experience foreign language anxiety from time to time, please note I am not vouching for group meetings to safeguard your communication where you may leverage the participation of another person to relieve your stress and preserve the flow of the dialogue. Fundamentally, you need to be reminded of the critical distinction between speaking fluently and connecting effectively in the essence of this book. It is critical to consider different conversational settings in a more nuanced way.

First and foremost, connection always requires energy. In simple terms, to bring energy requires each person to be intentional

MULTILINGUAL CONNECTORS

about understanding the other person and making the experience positive within the talk and, even better, beyond. Eventually, the energy needs to be exchanged and reciprocated for connection to emerge. Do you feel sometimes that despite being surrounded by lots of people, you can't make a genuine connection with any of them? Yet other times, even with a large group of people, most participants including you are very present and actively participating, there is an intense feeling of mutual energy exchange? Conversely, have you ever been in what seemed to be an intimate and engaging conversation with one person, but ultimately became draining and uncomfortable? If so, I hope you have at least had a single unforgettable one-on-one conversation where you wished time hadn't passed so quickly. It is true that some people are drains rather than fountains. They deplete, bore and de-energize and even worse, make you feel discouraged and demoralised should you be discussing some exciting prospects and goals. With these people, every second feels like hours. Hopefully, you have crossed paths with some amazing people you wish you had met earlier. With this in mind, do remember quality conversations can take place anywhere, between your relatives, friends and strangers, with someone native-speaking or else, in private and public settings, with an individual or group. It is possible for you to engage in deep conversations with a group and drain your energy with one individual. Your experience will ultimately be determined by how the conversation is set up and led by the people participating. Not only can the topic(s) influence the flow, how you and the other people conduct yourselves in the process can profoundly impact the vibration and chemistry between you.

DAISY WU

According to an interview featured in Babbel, a renowned languages and linguistics magazine, non-native speakers typically feel less pressured during conversations in the company of other non-native speakers, even when their peers are more fluent in the target language. Acknowledging this phenomenon which possibly mirrors our shared experiences, you must not underappreciate the other individual(s) participating in the same conversation as someone to simply buffer your nervousness, fill the awkward pauses or enhance your comprehension. Particularly, when you are on your own in a conversation, you don't have access to the perspective from another person, which can enrich the conversation dynamics and open your horizons. Understanding the premises of connections re-emphasized above, high-energy interactions between two people will not necessarily be diluted with another individual joining, provided that person exudes energy at the same or higher level.

'What if the other people joining the conversation talk over and outshine me, when they are more well-spoken and knowledgeable?' If a thought like this ever crosses your mind, it is a sign that you already contemplate the incoming meeting as a showground to fulfil your own agenda, often with the desire to be recognized and valued for your competency. This is the way many people view and approach networking, in professional contexts typically, which also increases their aversion towards this activity. Yet the previous paragraph should serve as a reminder of the mindset check on whether you genuinely view anyone in the meeting as conversation partners, who are your comrades to co-create valuable experiences with, rather than competitors to outperform. Meeting with more than one individual at once allows you to help others build community and in doing so, for yourself. Don't underestimate anyone's role in a conversation, especially that of your own! Even when you are only a new acquaintance to everyone else, you still can contribute to make the dialogue unforgettable and eye-opening for you all so that one day when these people recall the encounter, they will have you in mind and appreciate your presence.

I hope you will take some time to reflect on the nuanced perspectives above in light of your own experiences before navigating your next decision before or during a meet-up. When you think win-win, you will become more receptive and adaptive to a variety of conversational settings and capable of making the best out of it for yourself and others. Your attitude is the key to unlock the experiences you desire.

THE ALTERNATIVE TO TURNING UP IN PERSON

The expression 'out of sight, out of mind' can create the impression that if you do not show up regularly, ideally in person, others will forget you. If that is the impression you get from the paragraphs above, I should remind you that in common definitions, the act of showing up is to 'make someone or something conspicuous or clearly visible' where the outcome appears more defined than the methods. Your visibility and memorability will not be significantly impacted by limited in-person interaction in the digital age we all live in, so long as your online persona serves you in the right direction, as an expression and extension of you in multiple dimensions.

Research shows people generally display greater confidence in reading and writing compared to listening and speaking in a foreign language. This again makes the online realm the ideal place for non-native speakers in terms of impression management, as they have greater control over the outbound communication compared to instantaneous communications involving in speaking and listening.

A lot of people did not recognize I was a non-native English speaker from my social media content until they got to speak with me and I openly introduced my background. This isn't to suggest you hide an important part of your identity in a tactical way but a reminder to leverage the time and space the online realm affords for you to express yourself, allowing you to leverage your strengths.

Social media can be leveraged to manage others' impression of you to promote your personal brand. At its core, personal branding isn't about attempting to carve a new identity. Rather, it is in essence a deliberate exercise with the objective of promoting and highlighting your strengths and individuality in multiple dimensions that otherwise may not be seen by others. Therefore, personal branding is not a responsibility and right exclusive to celebrities and authorities, but an imperative for the Multilingual Connectors who wish to be better known, appreciated and valued in their network.

The benefits of extending your online persona also translate into what marketing strategist and author Ann Handley terms as 'pre-union' wherein you already know a person online before you finally get to meet in person. Giving others a slightly deeper glance into you adds colour and depth to the impression they

MULTILINGUAL CONNECTORS

form about you. This is the magic recipe for rapid rapport and accelerated connection with those you meet in person for the first time as your discovery about each other already started ahead of your meet-up, meaning you've already established a ground of commonality and interest as your foundation for connection.

Staying up to speed with our network via social media helps you navigate the realm of opportunities, and how to provide value to them. This can be as simple as sharing an event that may be of their interest, or make introductions to opportunities through private messaging. There is intrinsic value in this habit which makes it easier to connect with others at an emotional level. Be it career pivots, achievements or other life events significant to your connections, simply remembering these and mentioning them to the other person when you meet and reconnect demonstrates you have interest in that person and a strong intention to connect and stay connected. Every time I am recognized by a new face as 'the Daisy often sharing great content online', 'the Daisy who is very active in events' and 'the Daisy who does a lot of cool things', I usually smile ear to ear from the heart because it really means something to me that there are people watching my journey from near and far.

With the above scenario being an example, while you naturally wish to stay at the front of other's thoughts and consideration, in practice you will get the desirable experience and outcomes from connecting by implementing the wisdom of Zig Ziglar: 'You can have everything in life you want, if you will just help other people get what they want.'

DAISY WU

NO FILTER

The preceding chapter guides you to evaluate your network after you have entered each other's world and gotten to know each other better. While I introduce some important categories of people who can profoundly impact your life trajectory, you can rarely find any hard-fast rule or definitive criteria with respect to industry, gender, age, experience, race and ethnicity, whatever you would normally include in your considerations. Here is the paradox, the more prescriptive you are about who you want to connect with, including the particular individuals you know, the harder it is to find the connection you envisage in the first place. To clarify, there is nothing inherently problematic about having a premeditated matrix for any prospective connection. Rather, it helps to further define your ideal connections from demographics to psychographics. Whether these criteria are subjective and objective, don't discount people just because they don't immediately meet your criteria. You could be missing out on great connections because you're limiting yourself.

To illustrate, I have seen people leaving networking functions shortly after scanning the room and speaking to a few people only briefly. Sometimes they did not want to stay because they couldn't immediately find people who had aligned interests with them or specific background or profile they had hoped to find. Perhaps they did their due-diligence beforehand and showed up with the expectation of meeting someone who fit their criteria yet things didn't pan out as they'd wished.

The inherent limitations of criteria are also well exemplified in the pairing process of professional mentoring programs.

MULTILINGUAL CONNECTORS

With no guarantee for a 'perfect match' as per the pre-established matrices, the matching is typically based on demographic and occupation-related filters that define an individual's external characteristics. In my experience, most of the time I was paired with a mentor who appeared a great match according to my preferences and luckily, from a non-native speaking background whose insights I would then especially value. Nevertheless, among those seemingly good matches, the ones who I remain actively in touch with are few and far between months and years after the program ended. While I made a conscious decision to enter a professional relationship, I also secretly wished for a connection with the mentor on a personal level, though this did not happen in all mentorships I encountered.

I have had similar experiences in other professional settings too. In all fairness, the conventional labels such as industry, job title, organisation name, ethnicity and linguistic background at best guided me towards the solutions to some of my problems, including gaining career insights and referrals. Yet realistically speaking, a mechanical filter as such does not sift through a person for magnetic personality traits, inspiring and relatable life stories and wisdom, all of which are indispensable ingredients for deep and meaningful connections.

Type a few key words into the LinkedIn user search bar and see how many results pop up, and among them whose profile you would be interested to click into first. Consider who you'd be drawn towards without being guided by whether they pop up first or by their number of mutual connections or their appearance? You would probably conclude the filters are only helpful to a limited extent. Since each of us has our own unique life experiences, interests, and worldviews, how could a few labels possibly do us full justice? How much more could a well-written profile really serve us? Fundamentally, what these external labels cannot identify and filtrate is an individual's personality, character, values and goals, all of which are critical determinants of the chemistry between you that you will only find out when you have interacted with them. As for goals and visions, you should not pre-empt or pre-meditate anyone's vision based on his or her external identities, especially if you have other aspirations than the occupation-related. Not every engineer would aspire to design award-winning high-rise buildings. An accountant could also have music talent and dream of releasing albums. The examples are endless when you disregard commonly used filters.

The side effect of obsessing over your criteria can be further explained by the functioning of a bundle of nerves in your brain called the reticular activating system (RAS). Once you have well-defined and emotionalised goals programmed into the subconscious mind, the RAS triggers a mechanism that searches and filters the information you need for your conscious tasks. As you focus on ticking the boxes for who you meet and connect with, you send signals to your mind which is already occupied with the premeditated outcomes. While RAS may play out to help you get what you desire, in this instance, leading you to the 'right people' as per your standards and fulfilling your objectives behind connecting, you should also recognize the flip side of it in order to command its power to your advantage. To explain my point, when you zero in on pursuing a specific outcome that is based on meeting a particular type of person which will comply with your specific criteria, you limit your mental space for alternatives

MULTILINGUAL CONNECTORS

which your RAS may qualify as irrelevant information in your subconscious. In practical terms, this may result in you missing opportunities to connect with someone you unconsciously disqualify. It is likely that some of the best serendipitous encounters took place where you would least expect them.

Considering this, you should also be cautious of boxing yourself into any locations or occasions under the forces of your RAS. Keep in mind that the RAS only searches the subconscious information to assist the tasks at hand or to reinforce what you already believe but does not interpret if the task or belief really serves you. If you believe you can gain quality career insights from a professional with over twenty years of experience in your field via an industry mentoring program, your RAS may lead you towards that kind of person but does not decide whether such criteria may let you access the right career advice. How many times have you decided whether or not you should continue the dialogue with someone promptly after doing preliminary research or an introduction? Your obsession with fitting people into your matrices can cause you to jump the gun and pass the opportunity of connecting with someone truly good to know!

It is tempting to wait for the perfect opportunity, the right time, right place and right people or any other manifestation of alignment or perfection on your own terms. Yet as you wait for the stars to align and hold onto all your criteria uncompromisingly, you may just lose out on precious time and countless opportunities that may not appear in alignment in foresight but could turn out the opposite in hindsight. Prime your mind to give serendipity a chance, give others a chance and ultimately, yourself a chance!

CHAPTER 9

MAKE TIME YOUR FRIEND

"Time is more valuable than money. You can get more money, but you cannot get more time." — Jim Rohn

While it is worth investigating whether it usually takes a long period of time to forge meaningful relationships as many may believe, authentic connection goes far beyond trading time and resources. In essence, connection is an energy exchange which requires you and the other's emotional and spiritual investment and dedication, not just the physical or material. Provided this, time remains a pivotal variable in the formula for connections. Many high-achieving Multilingual Connectors I know have a demonstrated ability to prioritize and focus their energy strategically to take advantage of a host of opportunities. They also develop effective habits of setting and tracking goals.

Time is the great equaliser for all of mankind, as author and motivational speaker Jim Rohn well identified. Everyone has 24 hours in a day, 7 days a week, totalling 168 hours each week, regardless of one's social status. So many non-native speaking immigrants including myself and possibly you right now, can feel they are spread too thin living abroad where time management is integral. Other than the additional efforts to communicate well in a foreign language, we are no different from our native-speaking counterparts who also need to manage different priorities. There is no resource more finite than time. A good handle of time as your most valuable asset is key to your success in relationship building.

However much you have on your plate and however you feel about managing it all while contemplating the feasibility of adding a new task or goal, you shouldn't see time constraints as a necessary evil with a lack mentality. Nor should the passage of time be viewed as a rigid hurdle in your efforts to attain certain goals. In financial investment, you should know the importance of return on investment and the possibility of generating wealth from a small amount of equity investment and using leverages (i.e. borrowed money to increase your return on investment). When it comes to time management, these concepts and principles are translatable, which I will further elaborate.

MAKE TIME FOR THE IMPORTANT

As the world is getting busier and busier, it can feel as if you are too caught up and overwhelmed in the daily bombardment of errands and information through the Internet. Despite the busyness, do you feel drained and frustrated spending too much time managing trivial stuff or responding to crises? Perhaps you rate yourself as competent in terms of checking things off on your to-do list and managing emergencies, but do you ever feel you've not achieved anything of real significance? Do you often wish you could spend more time with somebody you care to connect deeper with?

If you relate to those feelings, chances are you do not fully understand the differences between urgency and importance or how they interplay. You need to appreciate that among the tasks you need to manage, there are some tasks that are directly relevant to your goals, and there are the ones you must attend to simultaneously in order to facilitate these activities. For example, if you want to be more efficient in forging connections via networking events, you need to think about making time to attend these events in the first instance, which may extend into improving your productivity so that you do not need to frequently work overtime and miss the social functions after business hours. This is why I need to discuss time management here within a broader context. Good command of time and priorities in one arena of life will have flow-on effects in the others. The saying 'how you do anything is how you do everything' deserves a place here. Those who manage their priorities well in other arenas are far more likely to fare well in managing their relationships than those less organised and cognisant in time management.

> *"Productivity is never an accident. It is always the result of a commitment to excellence, intelligent planning, and focused effort."* —Paul J. Meyer

MULTILINGUAL CONNECTORS

The former U.S President Dwight D. Eisenhower developed the Eisenhower Matrix, a prioritisation and time-management framework. It has four quadrants to categorise tasks defined by urgency and importance. Generally, urgent tasks require prompt action to fix the problem with a narrow and short-term focus. They often arise unexpectedly, catch you off guard and tend to interrupt or even derail you from what you are doing at the moment. Important tasks are those which propel you towards your long-term goals and make you feel fulfilled upon accomplishing. They require thoughtful planning and organisation and demand your continuing focus. Although some urgent tasks can also be important, many people simply equate urgency with importance or cannot tell them apart at all.

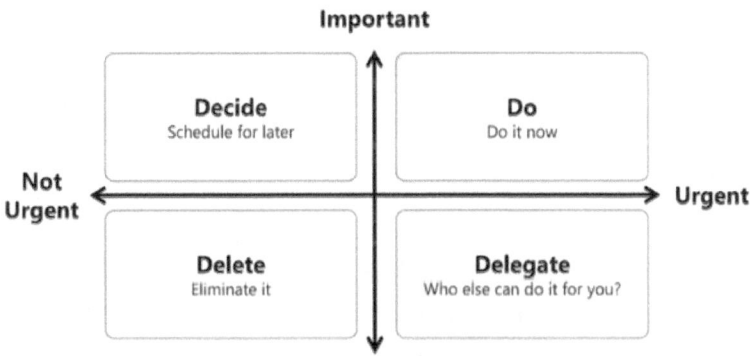

The Eisenhower Matrix (Credit: Idea to Value)

If you subscribe to the philosophy of this book, you will generally consider building connections as important. Within this arena, here is how you can apply this matrix to refine and optimise where you dedicate your precious time and energy:

- **Quadrant One (urgent and important):** The tasks in this quadrant demand your immediate attention such as pressing deadlines, crises, emergencies and errands postponed to the last minute. Stress and burnout are the common consequences of spending too much time here. I always remember the bitterness when I must pass an event to meet a deadline usually resulting from factors not entirely in my control. Being trapped in 'getting things done' mode is not a sustainable way to function, especially when the perceived importance is largely driven by how much your output matters to other people with a vested interest in you.

- **Quadrant Two (important but not urgent):** These tasks do not have an urgent deadline but require your ongoing input as they build up towards your important personal goals in the long run. I consciously dedicate time to this big picture quadrant. Rarely do I practically have pressing deadlines to nurture connections of specific types or forge any bond with a sense of urgency, which can make this cause of action feel mechanical and inauthentic. Despite this, I do prime my mind for building authentic relationships with like-minded people who nurture, inspire and expand me and this governs my decisions on time management. Book writing is another personal example because it provides an outlet to distil my experience and thoughts and translate them in ways that can give guidance and inspiration to other people. To facilitate the previous two activities, I also give English learning its fair share in Quadrant Two to keep refining my skills as a non-native speaker. As Quadrant Two tasks are not urgent, you need to decide if and when to schedule them for later, which should not equal excessive procrastination in any event. You need to strategically integrate these activities into your schedule in conjunction with those in the other quadrants and seek to maximise your time on Quadrant Two by all means.

- **Quadrant Three (urgent but not important):** Stephen Covey, the author of *The 7 Habits of Highly Effective People* observes many people spend most of their time on this quadrant. The key distinction from Quadrant One (urgent and important) is that Quadrant Three keeps you occupied but doesn't particularly help you to approach your goals, either short- or long-term. Typically, these tasks can be inconsequential meetings popping up on your schedule, unexpected phone calls, text messages and people dropping in for chit-chats or queries. In a networking setting, this could be an acquaintance or random person who walks over to strike up a conversation which interrupts you from approaching the person you need to speak to. To avoid the frustration these tasks can often bring you, you must learn to work smarter to avoid these tasks as much as possible, either by delegating or setting boundaries.

- **Quadrant Four (not urgent and not important):** These are distractions which hinder you from doing what matters for your long-term goals, and can range from social media browsing, shopping, partying, reading irrelevant emails and content. While time for entertainment and retreat is important for well-being, for the sake of accomplishing what is important to you, don't excessively and unconsciously engage in such disruptive activities. In respect to socialising and networking, you should be able to discern the activities and engagements that belong to this quadrant and those that don't. I consciously limit my commitment to social gatherings where I cannot find my feet in superficial conversations and/or low-energy uninspiring people. I am also mindful of staying in unintelligent conversations for too long. By unintelligent I do not imply the participants have low intellect but rather, the conversation being emotionally and spiritually unnourishing which are often based around gossiping, chitchatting or even worse, politicking and naysaying.

The Eisenhower Matrix gives you a clear framework for making decisions and in doing so, fast-track and eliminate some recurring and draining decisions – as long as you identify and zero in on your priorities, which should then dictate your choices. In the literature showcasing this matrix, the recommended responses to different tasks are often encapsulated in the 4D's, namely 'do, decide, delegate and delete' for Quadrant One to Four respectively. Common to all, you may have noticed that saying 'no' to things that are not conducive to achieving your goals and values is a key premise to capitalise on this model.

Foundational to your ability to say no and set boundaries for your important activities is whether you have clear directions in life built upon strategically set visions, goals and values.

If you find yourself easily caught up in the affairs and whims of other people and have an emerging sense of being a cog in the machine and exploited, it is likely that these people notice or worse, take advantage of your lack of direction, in the form of commitment to your personal goals or else. Such observation could legitimise you doing tasks for them rather than yourself. It is therefore imperative that you demonstrate high commitment to goals that matter to you as it shows you are spending your time in more meaningful and important ways than serving them. I believe saying no does not always equal disrespecting other people's priorities as a potential source of distraction. Your internal dialogue can affect what you project externally. Many of my most important goals are not self-serving which revolve around building positive impacts in the community, so I would never pre-empt or accept the image of a selfish person when defending my boundaries.

Saying 'no' is imaginably not the easiest thing to do or even think for many people, including myself once upon a time. Yet I have managed to gain a sense of confidence and control in my life as I've increased my time working on the not simply urgent but important tasks. The long-term emotional rewards outweigh the initial sense of resistance and reservation. From my experience, those truly like-minded connections will remain my comrades and champions even if I do not say yes to them more than once and my rejection sometimes leads to their disappointment for a short period of time. As I showcase my wins and the values I have created in the community, some of them could tell I am spending my time in a meaningful way. From there, they will respect my time and priorities more, be more understanding and accommodating.

Would you rather be constantly a utility for predominantly others' interest or regaining control over your life in the pursuit of your own dreams and aspirations? The call is yours.

DAISY WU

SET THE RIGHT GOALS TO ACHIEVE GOALS

"If you fail to plan, you are planning to fail!" — Benjamin Franklin

Although I don't need to reiterate the importance of having goals, attaining goals in the envisaged timeframe remains a challenge for many. As far as I am concerned, the solution is well encapsulated in the famous quote above. On the notion that 'a goal properly set is halfway reached', effective goal setting enables you to visualise and emotionalise your dreams, gives you clarity on the due actions, lets you measure progress and keeps you accountable to overcome resistance.

A lot of you would have been introduced to SMART goals in self-help resources to help ensure objectives are attainable within a certain time frame. However, whilst the SMART framework has its practical application in goal getting, it does not put the goal definition in context to first establish whether it is the appropriate goal to set to effectively spur on progression and transformation. In other words, it may help you achieve the goals defined in accordance with the framework but does not pinpoint whether you have pursued the right goals which help you to achieve your ultimate visions and objectives. Hence, on its own, the SMART framework cannot take you far and may even stagnate your progress. To give an example, if you set a goal to attend at least five networking events in your field with over twenty attendees within the next six months, with the ultimate objective of connecting with like-minded and resourceful people

MULTILINGUAL CONNECTORS

to collaborate on work projects. The goal, even when accomplished, may only elevate you to a wallflower who merely shows up at the mingling but not necessarily building relationships during and after to drive your agenda. Even if you have ticked the boxes by attending a minimum of five industry events to put yourself in front of people, you may still end up not moving any closer to your objective of finding project partners. In contrast, if you hold yourself accountable for at least five coffee chats as a follow-up of the five events you attend over these months, you will challenge yourself more to forge meaningful connections via the mechanical networking process.

From the example above, it is clear that unless goals can lead to a higher level of fulfilment, not even formulating them in the SMART framework guarantees completion. To tackle this, self-help author Bob Proctor introduces the ABC framework to explain how to set goals correctly. The ABC goal model categorises goals into A-Type, B-Type and C-Type:

A-Type goals are the goals you know how to achieve because you have already done them in the past. Therefore, they are also the exact goals that will ensure you stay where you are as they keep on producing similar results at the standards you have already been achieving. If you set a goal to attend ten events each year and talk to people in your non-native language and achieve it this year, next year it will be an A-Type goal if you aim for the same.

B-Type goals are goals that you have not yet achieved but will not cause you to question your ability to achieve them someday. They are only a level up from the A-Type goals. In the above example, initiating a coffee chat to explore collaboration opportunities may not be something you have done before but you will figure out the right ways eventually as you step out to start testing your invitation messages and navigating conversations. I used to have a B-Type goal of teaching in university tutorials. Speaking semi-impromptu in English in front of students, many of whom were native speakers, was initially a little daunting, not to mention I had no prior teaching experience. Yet I knew I should be able to do it after some preparation based on my current English skills and knowledge in this subject as a former student.

C-Type goals are those you have not done before and have no idea how to reach them from where you are. They are something you daydream about which not only excite you but as a hurdle criteria, scare you and can briefly set you on a journey of doubt or imposter syndrome since they can appear as though they are fantasies compared to your starting position. Note, a C-Type goal does not necessarily have to be as grand or radical as becoming your home country's president and improving the citizens' quality of life. It just needs to feel very bold and unrealistic in contrast to your current state and something you truly feel inspired by and, to meet the principal criteria: you do not have a tiny clue how to approach it here and now. Now I have done English public speaking via local industry events and podcast interviews and know they are no longer C-Type goals because none of them passes the fundamental test. Being a world-known best-selling author and international speaker to transform the lives of skilled immigrants meet the criteria and emotionalise me day by day and as I see the aforementioned speaking engagements pave my way to it.

Neither A-Type or B-Type goals are the arenas you want to play in for significant growth and progress, though they do still

MULTILINGUAL CONNECTORS

have their place in your development. As you achieve more and more B-Type goals, over time these goals automatically become A-Type goals which cease to stretch and expand you. By nature, they are framed within what you know or believe you can already do. Since they don't move you much further from the status quo, you are also unlikely to imagine feeling extremely rewarded and fulfilled upon achieving them. Therefore, these goals will not sustainably keep you inspired or motivated to take conducive actions.

With the ABC goal setting model, to have the context to frame and assess your goals, one thing to note is that you should only concentrate on what you want to achieve and why you want it so much. When setting a goal, most people are first concerned about if and how they can achieve it. When you place too much focus on figuring out the how's, you are prone to become less convicted about the goal and convince yourself you should probably not even start dreaming about something impossible to achieve at the first sign of setback. You need to pay more attention to the what and importantly your why to reinforce the belief in the meaning of the dream coming true, and the how will reveal itself. While this may sound like the law of attraction playing out, which many of you have heard of, the underlying psychological mechanism is actually termed as the reticular activating system (RAS) that the former chapter introduced. When a regularly emotionalised and visualised C-Type goal is programmed into your subconscious mind, your RAS system will constantly search the subconscious for the information you need for the task at hand. It keeps you alert to the people, platforms, channels and opportunities you may have previously turned a blind eye to or have newly entered your life.

I often hear people from different industries say it is hard to find a suitable avenue to connect with the 'right people', even when they have time to spare. Given the principle around the RAS, many people have evidently not leveraged this mental model which they are likely unaware of. When I had only just started at university, I would always think about getting good grades and landing a decent job before graduation to make my parents proud. I did not completely disrespect the fact that these goals were ambitious given I was a non-native speaker in a top-ranked university and fresh in my industry, but I did not let myself think about how challenging it would be even before learning about the RAS. It was simply a waste of mental energy to keep worrying about what may not work out which may only convince myself out of trying things that may unlock some opportunities. Not only did I sign up for student clubs and industry associations to stay tuned with events, I also got into the habit of using social media for professional networking early in my degree. Very likely under the influence of RAS, a series of opportunities emerged: as I kept meeting people who motivated me to expand my comfort zone, later I took on a few committee roles at non-profit organisations to host professional networking functions even before my own job offer landed. Within a year, the stars aligned in the lead up to my first construction job right at the end of my second year.

All you need to do is, dream bigger and trust in the process! Time will tell!

For reasons explained above, the SMART framework can be an instrumental complement to give your A-, B- and C-Type goals more granularity for the ease of execution and tracking.

MULTILINGUAL CONNECTORS

The criteria in SMART goals are commonly attributed to the Management by Objectives (MBO) concept in Peter Drucker's book *The Practice of Management*. The SMART stands for Specific, Measurable, Achievable, Relevant, and Time-Bound. This widely adopted approach reduces generalities and ambiguities in the goals to set a clear timeline to achieve concretely defined milestones and enable you to track progress.

S – **Specific:**

Specificity is a solid start with a clear identification of what you want to accomplish exactly. As the 'what' question may still elicit a general and vague response, you should consider it in the context of some other 'w' questions:

- What – What needs to be achieved – ranging from both the end outcomes and the enabling steps. Be as detailed as possible.
- Who – Identify the key persons that need to be involved to achieve the goal and who is most responsible for each step to achieve it. This not only applies to group projects. Carefully think about who you know or need to connect with to help you reach where you need to go.
- Where – There can be a location or occasion to approach your end goal. Identify any as either milestones or the final destination.
- Which – Identify the resources or limits involved. This can be beneficial to establish the practicality of your goal. For instance, if you wish to speak on industry panels but you never did so or have any existing connection to make referrals, then it may be identified as a present hurdle to help you

formulate the next steps.

M – Measurable:

How will you know when the goal is accomplished? Here, you make a goal more trackable. Consider the specific tasks in the lead up to that goal with the above parameters in mind for specificity. The goals should contain quantifiable and/or tangible criteria to assess how well you are approaching them.

A – Achievable

Your goal needs to be realistic and attainable to have efficacy. Note this parameter is meant to inspire motivation rather than discouragement. If you do not possess the necessary skills, resources and tools or have convenient access to any of these from your connections, consider the necessary actions to attain them. When an achievable goal is set, it should prompt you to identify previously overlooked opportunities or resources to move you closer to it. In other words, it should remain possible even with a stretch to your capabilities and mindset.

R – Relevant

By considering its relevance, you assess on a continuous basis whether the goal is meaningful to you based on your own matrix and if it fits in with the broader objectives. It ensures your cause of action begins with the end in mind and does not deviate much from the track that leads to it. Even though there may be a myriad of ways to fulfil your objectives, you still need to come up with ways to measure how the goal relates to the steps you need to achieve your milestones. For instance, connecting with the professionals from your own cultural background in a foreign city may initially appear not closely aligned with your main objective of building a multicultural professional network. Yet if you examine closely, the process of attaining that goal should let you build up your social skills that are transferable in other professional settings; it may also provide you with access to other people's cross-cultural network which you may leverage.

T – Time-Bound

Each goal should be set with a target date and the deadlines for all the deliverables are equally imperative. It is useful to have a realistic time frame with time constraints creating a sense of urgency and accountability but also with sensible deadlines that forge you ahead rather than deterring or derailing you from actions.

Applying the ABC Goal framework in conjunction with SMART goals provides a rather comprehensive and multi-dimensional context for setting and tracking goals. My one last piece of advice to safeguard your goal attainment would be to keep your goals with either yourself, or those who deserve a place in your dreams and aspirations and who can provide emotional and moral support along your growth paths. Taking the key lessons from a chapter earlier, you must heed the noises and negative voices that can kill your dream in the cradle.

LET TIME RUN ITS COURSE

The great Albert Einstein famously referred to compounding interest as the eighth wonder of the world. Many of you should be familiar with the principle underlying the compounding effect which translates that small, smart choices consistently made will pay huge rewards. Productive and effective Multilingual Connectors are consistent with the good habits, disciplines and hard work in the form of small yet continuous actions. They are not addicted to instant gratification.

> *"Slow and steady wins the race."* — Aesop

The above expression from the fable *The Tortoise and the Hare* well summarises the essence of steady and continuous progress which will outpace sporadic and inconsistent efforts. At many points in your life, you might meet individuals who seem to be going fast and far in that moment but if you keep observing their trajectory, it is possible that months or years later, you cannot find them anywhere ahead of you. Some people take action upon spurs of inspiration and whim but they do not keep up once motivation fades away. Many fail with thirty-day challenges, usually not making it past the initial week. According to Insightout Mastery, 25% will quit their New Year's resolutions within the first week of the year.

To help you better exploit the magic of compounding and overcome resistance to adopt a small change for good, I will introduce the habit stacking routine created by James Clear in his book *Atomic Habit*. It consists of augmenting new actions you want to adopt on top of what you already do and normally find enjoyable. Clear highlights how it can help you build routines you are able to show up for to get 1% better day by day with reduced risks of burnout or over exhaustion.

MULTILINGUAL CONNECTORS

I am not an advocate for any intensive training program or daily challenge for habit formation with the activities in target typically generating resistance. In this light, I've found habit stacking an effective technique in developing routines even when I feel unmotivated for the activity to reinforce a new habit. An example from myself is to integrate daily English learning routine into social media use. This way, I consciously browse and write posts online to build up my receptive and productive vocabulary. It also mitigates social media browsing as often an unfavourable Quadrant Four activity (not urgent or important) in the Eisenhower Matrix. In the same token, I also don't feel it is a stretch to write content using new vocabulary around the activities I enjoy, such as piano playing and networking.

On networking, habit stacking has broad applications for those yet to identify themselves as actively engaged. Instead of pushing yourself to attend events once every few days, you may just start by inviting acquaintances to the table of your routine weekend lunch or weekday coffee to ease into the habit of networking conversation. As another example, you may strike up a conversation with an unfamiliar face in a familiar setting you enjoy such as your office Friday drink, before talking to strangers and new acquaintances becomes more of a second nature.

Do not underestimate one tiny change whether you are seeking to keep your goals in sight or embrace new habits in reference to the abovementioned Eisenhower Matrix. The key is making showing up a habit and staying the course. As the general saying goes, 'success breeds success.' Often, these small changes also bring about flow-on and ripple effects whereby you become more incentivised to make another small change and then another.

DAISY WU

REAP WHAT YOU SOW

The Law of Harvest

'Whoever sows sparingly will also reap sparingly, and whoever sows generously will also reap generously.' — 2 Corinthians 9:6-11 NIV

In today's world, it is not uncommon for people to want the harvest without even dropping the seeds. You reap what you sow — that's how the Law of Harvest applies.

$$A = P(1 + \frac{r}{n})^{nt}$$

A = final amount
P = initial principal balance
r = interest rate
n = number of times interest applied per time period
t = number of time periods elapsed

The Compound Interest Formula (Credit: CalculatorSoup)

Furthermore, it is also evident from the above formula that the passage of time on its own will not be a magical solution for anybody if they don't first make the initial investment. Doing the minimum for your connections and prospects while expecting the maximum from them is not going to let you go far. It is quite easy to reach out when you are in need but it is comparatively more rare for people to invest in someone without expecting anything in return.

To illustrate the above phenomenon, a study led by MIT

researchers analysed friendship ties in a classroom of people aged between 23 to 38 who were asked to rank their closeness to each of their classmates. They were surprised that 94% of the subjects expected the other person to agree on the same ranking as they gave to that one but only 53% of the feelings were reciprocated. In other words, we sometimes overestimate our intimacy with some people. On this, you might recall an occasion where the other person you identified as a close contact and reached out to turned out not as responsive, enthusiastic or supportive as you anticipated them to be which made you feel hurt, disappointed and possibly confused. Part of the cause of this phenomenon can be people having different definitions of friendship and closeness. Clearly, some people, ignorant of this fact, are oblivious when they send out request for support without weighing up their own role and commitment in the relationship.

Are you in the habit of giving and investing or taking and expecting? 'Dig the well before you're thirsty.' In the spirit of this, prepare for what you need prior to needing it.

The underrated weak ties

The passing of time has the magic to evolve your relationship with a certain group of people in your network, termed by Stanford University sociologist Mark Granovetter as 'weak ties'. It refers to the people in your network who you know basically at best and have possibly met via a shared contact or worked with shortly. Note that the word 'weak' does not have negative connotations. It simply portrays the depth of your relationship in the moment which can evolve over time. The most comparative and common term for this group would be acquaintances, namely those people a person knows slightly but who are not close friends. An important finding in Granovetter's paper where he first introduced the concept of weak ties is that those with whom we are weakly associated are more likely to evolve in fields and areas other than our own and hence will get access to the information, knowledge and resources different from what we receive from our circles.

People who we do not know well or almost have forgotten have the potential to solve some of our problems or propel us into a breakthrough. This is because they may have the insights and network which are distinct from those we obtain from our usual circle or contacts, and which could be exactly what we need to solve the problems we have been stuck in. They can be someone you once crossed paths with during a networking event, a friend's birthday party or even a flight. Anyone you can think of can be a weak tie, whose network, knowledge or idea refreshes your outlook, gets you through a new door or inspires you to go in a direction outside of what you would normally consider. The possibilities are almost endless. Be conscious of keeping these people in the back of your mind when you need guidance, perspective and advice, seek introductions, inspiration and resources.

As stressed in the former section, it is not effective to passively wait for time to pass, waiting for the day when you might happen upon the jackpot in your circle of weak ties. To accelerate the connection one day and turn them into a friend, partner, referral or champion in times of need, you have to find ways to stay tuned and in loose touch with these people. Referring to the Law of Harvest, from a distance, you should stay in the mindset of giving and sowing. Keep your eyes on the ball for opportunities to provide value to these people before you ever need something from them.

MULTILINGUAL CONNECTORS

BYPASSING TIME

A marketing rule of thumb goes that it takes eight to twelve connections over a year to move from the initial introduction to a relationship. Often, we tend to believe relationships take a long period of time to nurture, especially the close and deep ones. In parallel, there are common notions as 'rapid rapport' and 'whirlwind romance' backed by countless real-life examples that serve as antidotes.

In the first chapter I introduced the foundational elements of likeability identified by author Tim Sande: friendliness, relevance, empathy and authenticity. Likeability is a subjective and vague concept premised on the positive attitude you invoke in other people. By being more personable, pleasant, and popular, all of which are forms of likeability, you will find it easier to connect and build trust within other people.

In practical terms, here are some of the critical habits you should cultivate to become exceptionally likeable:

1. Develop an optimistic attitude towards life – which leads to less cynicism and more relatability.
2. Speak with confidence and sincerity – say the words from the heart with a loving and pleasing tone.
3. Be an active listener – which entails a genuine interest in learning from other people's perspectives.
4. Have emotional agility and fortitude – do not overreact to situations, either positive or negative.
5. Be receptive and open-minded to others' ideas, including those you may disagree with.
6. Have pleasing facial expressions – smile a little bit more,

frown less and appear calm and collected instead of pulling a long face in negative events.
7. Make conscious efforts in seeking a positive lesson in challenges and setbacks.
8. Practise intentional gratitude – never take anyone and what they do for you as granted.
9. Be generous with praise – be specific, authentic, and sincere with your compliments and do not stop short of doing them simply because you believe the receivers may not care much about words of acknowledgement.

Time isn't your enemy or ally in absolute terms. It is in fact neutral, much like money. You simply need to make conscious decisions about what to do with it. Though it is finite in practical terms for each individual, it is also possible to be created. As discussed from multiple angles, time has the power to transform our network and ourselves as individuals as well as the bonds between us. Nevertheless, time is not always the hurdle to grow good and meaningful connections. Command your time before it commands you!

CHAPTER 10

THE LESS YOU COMMUNICATE, THE MORE MISTAKES YOU MAKE

"The single biggest problem in communication is the illusion that it has taken place." — George Bernard Shaw

There are whole industries dedicated to correcting mistakes in a foreign language and communication more generally. Aside from the technical knowledge and skills needed to avoid mistakes, training and education also extends to how to recover and keep going after making a mistake. In foreign language education and personal development industries, the notion that mistakes are inevitable is imparted widely to motivate people into action to step out of their comfort zone and learn from the mistakes. Nonetheless, in the same backdrop, there is a significant category of mistakes which is much less discussed: the mistake of under-communicating as the exact opposite of overcommunicating – where one deliberately communicates more than is normal or generally considered necessary to emphasise important information. Typically, people entertain and analyse the cost of making mistakes when taking action but much more rarely do they consider the mistakes they might make due to the action not taken.

The concept of under-communicating assumes that the information is delivered ineffectively to the receiving party. In work settings, communication difficulties can undermine productivity and efficiency and result in missed deadlines, unmet expectations and an overall drop in staff morale. At a broader interpersonal level, a lack of communication can have far-reaching and long-lasting consequences for any relationship, leading to misunderstandings and conflicts and causing two or more parties to disconnect from each other.

Often, the lack of communication takes the form of inaction where one avoids communication as a result of fear or reservations. In famous American politician Chuck Schumer's words, inaction is 'perhaps the greatest mistake of all.' While looking at the barriers causing under-communication, it is also noteworthy that one can also fall short of communicating certain things in certain ways because he/she does not fully recognize the benefits it could bring. On this, there is an unknown quote that goes, 'Without communication there is no relationship.' It speaks to the importance of effective communication being open, honest and transparent for building and maintaining a good connection with somebody else. It is the most basic of all human needs to understand and be understood.

MULTILINGUAL CONNECTORS

With the end goal in mind, namely connecting with others meaningfully in the realm of opportunities, I will delve into several types of communication mistakes that stem from under communication and how to mitigate these mistakes especially if you identify as non-native speaking.

REACHING OUT MAKES YOU STRONGER

In an earlier chapter, I explained the importance of delegation and interdependence. As much as the concept is widely illuminated in studies and literature, it is yet to be commonly understood and practised. In *How to Delegate Work Effectively & Be A Successful Leader*, Brian Tracy identifies ego as a key barrier to delegation. Do you tend to think if you need to seek out external support you are less capable than others? Do you hesitate to ask for help and support because you don't want to be perceived as incompetent? Strikingly, according to Merissa King in *Social Chemistry*, there is a large body of research showing that people who are less resourceful are less likely to ask for help because it strengthens feelings of powerlessness. This in turn makes them less optimistic and confident in the face of risks and challenges.

Though it may appear as though projecting a lack of confidence, it actually takes great confidence to be truthful about what you don't know and ask for help and advice. You should not see asking for support and delegation as a sign of weakness and incompetence. No one knows everything and you don't know what you don't know. The ego and complacency will not do you any good. According to Brian Tracy, the average person today is working at 50% of capacity due to underutilization of delegation skills. The data should give you a strong reason to tap into the unused 50% potential to increase you and your team's productivity. Provided this, you should also leverage delegation in the faith of expanding your references on how other people apply the language to solve the problem which you may already have your own solution to.

Understanding the essence of delegation and interdependence given the ultimate aim of improving results and relationships in a win-win situation, you should reach out more often. Working as a junior, I had limited authority to pull resources and delegate. That said, whenever I could not fully delegate, I would still seek to apply its essence to teamworking and get things done better and faster. When a manager took me under her wings on a new project, I initially let her help me draft up important emails to the key stakeholders. Even though I actually felt technically competent in the language and subject matter to give it a go on my own, I would usually take advantage of the onboarding phase. Why? I could have worded it in my own way but my outputs edited by the manager may not exactly be what she would have put down in the first place. Apart from the word use, sentence structure and actual contents, I would pay more attention to the overall flow of the message and how they connected to the needs and wants of stakeholders on key subject within a few lines. As I followed suit and gradually became more independent, I would still not hesitate to capitalise on such learning experience when necessary, such as in a high-pressure and high-stake situation. 'A mistake is not virtually a mistake until it gets out the door.' I took this advice onboard from our internal training and benefited from putting it into execution.

MULTILINGUAL CONNECTORS

In the above example, my relationships with my colleagues cemented in noticeable ways as our touch points increased with the passage of time. Not only did I become better versed in work matters, the frequent interactions naturally flew on to conversations highly beneficial to my professional development which I would otherwise not have accessed.

IT'S BETTER TO ASK FOR A FAVOUR THAN GIVE ONE

"He that has once done you a kindness will be more ready to do you another, than he whom you yourself have obliged." — Benjamin Franklin

While I always believe being a resourceful and supportive individual is instrumental to building connections, I also find myself strongly connected with those I have 'bothered' and 'troubled' for matters big or small. Noticeably, those who displayed a supportive gesture in the first instance pretty much let it carry through as I got the second 'yes' from them and so forth. In many instances, the favour I received was almost unconditional and unreciprocated which made me feel blessed as a foreigner with no close relative to lean on overseas. To a certain degree they also made me feel like an imposter and ponder what I had done to deserve all of these.

There is a psychological phenomenon termed the Ben Franklin effect to explain this. It is a cognitive bias and boils down to the idea that people get to like someone more after doing that person a favour, especially if they disliked that person or felt neutral toward them previously. The driving force is cognitive dissonance, a state of tension in which a person holds two psychologically inconsistent ideas, beliefs, attitudes or opinions. Under the Ben Franklin effect, the notion that one has done someone a favour contrasts their current negative or neutral attitude towards that person which produces cognitive dissonance. To resolve the discomfort, our minds trend towards self-justification, instead of confronting the mistake from supporting someone we don't like and unworthy of our favour. The easiest way to rationalize the favour done is to believe 'that person is good and deserving of the support and investment'.

Since the Ben Franklin effect is driven primarily by the desire to reduce cognitive dissonance, it works typically well in situations where others have negative, neutral or no preexisting attitude toward you. It can sometimes also work if the person you ask for a favour likes you moderately, so long as the scope of the favour in question outweighs the degree of their liking. Generally, in theory, the scope of the favour doesn't matter as much as the act of favour itself. Quite often, the increase in rapport comes from the fact that the other one has lent you a supportive hand, even if the favour is relatively minor. The effect of cognitive dissonance can overtime compound and make the subject more convicted to like the person receiving support and assistance again and again.

Intuitively, we may hesitate to reach out for support because the feeling of indebtedness to someone caused by both asking for and receiving the favour. Understanding the Ben Franklin effect, we should realise that when applied properly, this psychological technique can gain your favour or create greater rapport with others. Here are my advice suggestions to help you make good use of this technique:

1. **Have faith in others' willingness to help**:

   Studies show we tend to underestimate how much others are likely to help us. To explain this, when seeking assistance we focus on the expected cost of requesting favour while our potential helpers focus on the expected social cost of saying no, which most people want to avoid whenever possible. In other words, compared to sending a request, it actually is risker to decline a request. Therefore, whether it's soliciting a favour or building rapport, do not worry too much about exposing your intentions to the other person who, under normal conditions, is more concerned about the consequences of rejecting you.

2. **Be realistic with regard to who you approach and what's asked for:**

   You must be cognisant of your relationship with the potential helper. Generally, the scope of favour should be weighed up against quality of the relationship. Though it is possible to receive a huge favour from someone you barely know, at all times you have the duty to communicate the cost of the favour and why you believe it's in your (and sometimes both of your) best interest to have that person perform the favour.

3. **Leverage the power of reciprocity:**

   There is research evidence showing the likelihood of rejection decreases when we perform a favour for the other person first. Given the reciprocity effects, if you need to ask for a huge favour, it may be a good idea to start with a small favour that you can offer/perform for them first, before moving to a major request later.

4. **Practice gratitude:**

The power of gratitude cannot be overemphasised. It is an attitude, not just action. In other words, you not only have to express thankfulness to the other person after getting the support but even before you consider reaching out, get in the habit of expressing gratitude for the small things others do for you and/or someone else.

THE PROBLEM WITH OVER COMMUNICATING 'PERFECTION'

The problem with perfectionism cannot be overstressed. Though it is widely acknowledged perfection doesn't really exist, the inclination towards perfectionism is still commonly found as many individuals strive to present the best possible version of themselves in others' eyes. Comparatively, much less people display willingness to reveal their shortcomings, struggles and setbacks. Whilst I have no objection to self-promoting in the faith of serving others by showing our strengths, I believe we also have the responsibility to present ourselves in other dimensions as perfectly imperfect unique individual beings.

In the common interview question 'What are your strengths and weaknesses?', the weaknesses are perhaps the most nerve-wracking part. Though everybody has weaknesses, who wants to admit to them, especially in an interview where there is a strong desire for the interviewer to respect and notice your strengths? Successful candidates often approach such a question to demonstrate their self-awareness and growth orientation. My

MULTILINGUAL CONNECTORS

understanding around such interview techniques boils down to scripting your imperfections to connect with the audience in ways that demonstrate your drive and means to improve upon your imperfection in a way that is relevant and relatable to them.

In recent years, many people didn't realise English was my second language until they heard me speaking or came across my content, podcast and my book. Without looking further into my world, others would also tend to assume I migrated overseas early with a good language environment so it's a given for me to build a strong network in a culturally diverse community. Until I learnt to leverage thought leadership, people rarely appreciated where I came from and how far I'd come. As time passed, my achievements built up the pedestal many peers would put me on. I was also responsible for reinforcing the perception that mastering English as a second language and connection skills were almost effortless for me. I didn't realise such a persona could be a disservice to me until I failed to connect well with prospects when introducing my mentoring service to some non-native English speakers who were like past me. At first I was very confused when some prospective mentees didn't have any faith in my theory that you can thrive without speaking perfect English. I think this was mostly because they assumed I was coming from a vantage point they didn't have. Not only was it obscure to them that foreign language anxiety continues to affect me at different stages, they also didn't recognize the interpersonal challenges I still faced even after my language skills advanced, which created the impetus of my thought leadership. Initially most of my educational content for non-native speakers did not effectively reach and connect with the target audience. It took me many trials and tribulations to recognize the communication gap where I was falling short in connecting with the audience on the pains and struggles common to hundreds and thousands of non-native speakers at different levels.

Commonality is an essential ingredient for connection which largely dictates which parts of your vulnerable self to unveil. None of what I advise in this book would have validity without revealing the 'multi-dimensional me', the then shy and unconfident Chinese international student and all the inner battles and noises that are ongoing even when I appear high-performing and high-functioning. I've made a conscious decision on such self-disclosure in an open and transparent manner to show others I walk my talk in order to get to where I am today – a long way from where I began years back. I'm not just a name at the top of the charts and on the awards and accolades. Besides all of these, I'm also an ordinary human being with no background of privilege who experiences a spectrum of emotions in the ebbs and flows of life overseas. I could be seen as lucky – but before luck comes my way again and again, there comes failures, rejections and stagnation.

With the power of vulnerability already underscored, it is imperative to be cognisant of the context and the key objectives which determine what you communicate and how. Besides job interviews, in a wider setting, overcommunicating your weaknesses and challenges does you little good unless you give the audience a good reason to care and take action in your favour. Up to this point of the book, you should recognize the secret is that you can leverage imperfection as a superpower to connect: make it about them.

MULTILINGUAL CONNECTORS

MAKE SMALL TALK A BIG DEAL

'Hey, how are you?', 'Hi, how's things?', 'Did you have a nice weekend?' How do you feel about these polite greetings and conversation starters about unimportant or uncontroversial matters? Do they make it even harder for you to settle into a meeting with someone you barely know? Do you feel such dialogues are a waste of time and wish to avoid them as much as possible? Do you struggle to stay in the dialogue for even just a little while following such default preambles as 'I'm good…', 'Yeah it was nice …' A common term for such communication whose substance is inconsequential is small talk. Small talk is a social norm in many parts of the world, both eastern and western. By definition, it is the opposite of the important and crucial 'main conversations' around tasks, agenda, and strategies in a work setting. It is anything off-task because we're not discussing anything about the serious business.

Though studies show such casual informal conversation makes up almost one-third of adult conversation, for some people, small talk often feels like a clumsy dance which neither person knows how to lead. Depending on your own cultural background, you may likely experience 'cultural clash' in the way small talk is conducted in the foreign environment, which could include having such chatty conversation starters if you are not from a widely recognized small talk culture such as America and Australia. Cross-cultural small talk can also be an unexpected minefield where cultural misunderstandings and incorrect assumptions can backfire and make the attempt of bonding counterproductive. Small talk in a foreign language or culture can indeed be nerve-wracking, considering how well you speak the language on its own is already enough to intensify the fear of making mistakes and feeling of awkwardness.

For many, in any language, it may seem like small talk does no more good than filling up awkward gaps and silence before the main agenda is ushered in or the window appears for you to narrowly 'escape' from the encounter. While the aversion to small talk can come off as being awkward, shy, indifferent, antisocial, or even rude, small talk is popularly perceived as superficial and draining wherein questions and commentaries are either predictable and exhausting or poorly considered and a way to throw someone off guard. Despite this, self-help guru Dale Carnegie, the author of *How to Win Friends and Influence People* popularized the idea that small talk is an important business skill. To put this outlook into perspective, we need to re-examine the role of small talk.

Rather than just being a filler at the start or interval of a key agenda, small talk takes on special significance when meeting a new acquaintance as it allows you to size each other up in terms of how you conduct and present yourself. Remember the importance of first impressions and the types of communication going beyond the words introduced before, small talk is a big deal. When you are in business, it is also tempting to be task-oriented and get caught up in the 'getting things done' mentality as a way to meet competing demands. That said, there is the time and space for small talk as a means of easing in and out of the serious business conversation. It allows you to virtually 'limber up', a way of stretching emotionally and cognitively. As for its power to help people settle into crucial conversations, people naturally and subconsciously gravitate toward those who are similar and familiar. Therefore, small talk is an opportunity for you and the other person to discover commonalities in the off-task matters which portrays you in other ways than your professional identity. The common ground you navigated via small talk can enhance your likeability and familiarity for the ease of connecting and collaborating. It also provides the hook for you to develop an ongoing connection with this person, by establishing common grounds outside of the transactional and business-related context.

You should recall that our memories focus on how others made us feel more effectively than what we did and said in the interaction. This is the exact mental model you can capitalise on to make small talk your 'connection accelerator'. If you often scratch your head about finding a good topic to discuss, worry not because in the long run, the emotional experience you co-create with others has a more lasting impact than what you talk about and how well you express yourself. Instead, it is the feelings and emotions that we register in others' minds during such casual conversations that forms the hurdle or launch pad for the next point of contact and level of connection. In reference to our emotional experiences in the past and moment, we navigate the ground for deeper conversations and relationships in future: Does the other person make us feel comfortable enough to carry on the talk? Are they interested in us? Does that person seem easy to deal with? Am I welcome to express myself more in his or her company?

Obviously, not all small talk is the same. For any conversation to be constructive and productive, it largely depends on the people leading it. It is surely a defining quality of a Multilingual

Connector to turn small talk from a seemingly forced meaningless dialogue into a powerful social lubricator for better engagement and relationship building.

To transform small talk from an obligation to an opportunity to nurture connections, especially with the challenges stemming from the foreign language and culture, here is my advice on navigating cross-culture small talk:

1. **Bring high energy**:

'How are you?' 'I'm good …' 'Not too bad, yourself?' I'm sure among all the predictable responses, you have experienced different energy in the same words. Sometimes you can already hear the 'Monday blues' and indifference in the way they sound without looking the person in the face. In contrast, there would be someone else you know who consistently radiates with high energy even in such trivial small greetings. Your attitude is not only perceivable from how you sound. The whole suite of your non-verbal language also conveys your energy. To me, there is always a level just above the bottom line of politeness and decency which few people meet.

2. **Make the other person feel at ease**:

While not all the topics keep you interested and engaged, you should always do your best to make the dialogue a positive experience to make their day a little brighter. Wear a warm smile, look into the person's eyes and be active in responding, sharing your view and giving compliments or praises where you can.

3. **Leverage curiosity:**

The one thing that has helped me overcome my fear of small talk is to make it about the other person instead of myself. The

MULTILINGUAL CONNECTORS

top quality to keep you in the right direction is curiosity. People often wonder what to say to engage well in dialogues. From my point of view, to engage well doesn't just entail saying things of interest. A large part of good engagement is effective listening, which builds upon curiosity to gather information about others with an attitude to serve them. Rather than sweating about saying something interesting and relatable, you might simply be better off if you focus more on improving your ability to listen well and steer the conversation. The stress is off your shoulders as you learn to hand over part of the talk to the other person. Often people believe small talk is superficial and artificial - not if you make it about them, not if you are genuinely curious about them and exert conscious efforts to make it about them.

4. **Enjoy the process:**

There used to be a period where I struggled to find opportunities for small talk in an English-speaking country. Therefore, when my language environment improved I seized every opportunity as a practice ground. As a non-native English speaker, every time I managed to stretch myself a little by staying in the conversation a bit longer past the greeting and predictable 'weather commentary' and 'weekend check-in', I felt a sense of reward, from both making the attempt to express myself in the second language and also learning something new about the other person. To overcome the fear and reservations due to language skills, it is helpful to remember most people don't pay attention to or take too seriously what's actually being said in the process, compared to the overall experience which cannot be solely measured by the quality of language or conversation contents. In some settings, we are unlikely to meet the other person again or anytime soon,

so this also de-risks how you conduct yourself.
5. **Build up your cultural intelligence (CQ):**
CQ is an important quality introduced in Chapter 5. Cultural misunderstandings and incorrect assumptions can clearly impact budding relationships, either personal or professional and can sometimes have serious consequences. It is crucial to adjust expectations when learning to establish bonds in a culture where people's small talk appetites vary from the ones akin to yours. For instance, in my home country China, some people can be protective towards personal information when dealing with those they are not close to because they are concerned that the information may be used against them in a competitive environment.
6. **Be respectful:**
Developing cultural intelligence can serve you in this direction. More generally, we should stay observant in the process and be mindful of oversharing and overreaching as we probe other people's boundaries. Know when to call it a day when the other person displays an inclination to wrap it up, possibly because they need to move to more important errands, are starting to feel the stretch of further discussing the topic or simply do not wish to continue the dialogue. So long as you understand the nature of small talk, you should know better than to take any of such responses too personal. The last thing you would wish for is to let the shallow conversation backfire on you and undermine your opportunity for further meaningful connections should a negative impression be formed.

If you still carry a shadow of doubt about such informational dialogues that seemingly serve as a buffer to the main business and not leading us anywhere else, then I want to remind you that we may not connect the dots in the moment but possibly, in hindsight. It is a powerful habit to leverage small talk at work and during networking as fertile ground to seed and reap the hooks for connection. To draw some examples from my experience, knowing the hobbies, lifestyles and preferences of someone through small talk and coffee chats allows me to tailor future touch points around them, such as meeting the next time at that person's favourite restaurant in town, buying gifts from their preferred brands, or simply initiating topics of interest to them. A brief share of my latest experience on a project or networking function following routine greetings sometimes lends itself to further conversations with valuable insights which benefits my day-to-day job. From there, new opportunities emerge to work on exciting projects in and outside of my day job as my competency and interest become better known to the other person.

Small talk is a big deal with the potential of helping you convert the bigger deals, be it transactional or relational. For you to maximise the power of small talk as a Multilingual Connector, it is paramount to approach it with the right mindset and skill set. Don't think and play small!

CONNECTION OVER CONVENIENCE

A study at Stanford of 16,000 workers over COVID-19 discovered productivity can increase by 13% by working from home. In the past decade we have also witnessed a surge of digital communications and online services including mobile banking and meal delivery offering great convenience to our lives. Whilst there is ample evidence in support of productivity gains and work satisfaction via remote and hybrid working, many emerging from the recent pandemic seemed to realise the one thing they missed was authentic and genuine connections with other people, especially beyond their closest circle. Indeed, social distancing largely diminished the more intimate conversations with co-workers and acquaintances beyond the task-oriented messages on calls, emails and chat boxes. Studies before COVID-19 over a decade ago also proved our emotional attachment to other people deteriorates fast without face-to-face contact: feelings of closeness between family members and friends drop by over 30% after two months without gathering in-person, and almost 80% after five months of distancing.

Whilst people broadly report they have missed human connections during the pandemic, in adjusting to the 'new normal', there is still a degree of resistance to face-to-face contacts for non-clinical reasons. In today's fast-paced and competitive world post pandemic, more and more people are gravitating towards convenience at the sacrifice of connection. According to a report by Owl Labs in 2021, almost 70% of those who worked from home during the COVID-19 pandemic reported less stress in virtual meetings and identified hybrid working mode as an ongoing preference. As a non-native English speaker, I do appreciate some of the benefits of remote working. True, in virtual meetings and presentations, speaking could be guarded with scripts and outlines in a document we could navigate conveniently, alongside other forms of multi-tasking to enhance the accuracy of foreign language communication. Notwithstanding that, there is still a strong case for speaking with imperfection in person

MULTILINGUAL CONNECTORS

and impromptu, which can sometimes work even better than polished writing. How so? If you hide behind emails and texts, it will be harder for others to experience you at first hand. Since we human beings run fully on various senses, actually getting the voice and even better, meeting the person feels more enticing and grounding.

As the previous chapters already illuminated, you are not only defined by how well you speak or write, you are also evaluated by how you present yourself in your physical appearance, dressing style, body language and personality, all of which cannot be done in full justice through writing or virtual communications in general. The disrupted communication patterns caused by the COVID-19 pandemic also reinforces the idea that we are dulling our senses if emailing, messaging and video-calling is how we communicate for most of our day. If you want others to see and hear you better, question whether you have personally put enough effort to make it easier for others to do so.

With the role of small talk already discussed, increasing face-to-face contact widens the window for such seemingly trivial yet actually essential tribal babble to advance rapport and connection. In the post-COVID world there remains a population who prefer to work from home with the key objective of minimising small talk which they find draining and distracting. Regarding this outlook, while we normally will not have deep and intimate conversations in initial encounters and certain occasions, having multiple touch points with someone in person on a continuous basis does create ample opportunities to know each other better. True, the time saved from the chitchats, catch-ups and social functions may translate into productivity increase on timesheets.

However, in the meantime you may also be passing opportunities to build better connections with others. Using the techniques introduced before, it is possible to rescript your dialogue about increasing face-to-face interactions once you become a bit more intentional about leveraging those seemingly inconsequential and time-consuming interactions and reap the benefits.

Note that here I am not advocating for presenteeism or in-person meetings as the best possible way to connect and collaborate. What I vouch for is the mentality of exerting deliberate effort to make it easier for others to get to know you personally and professionally, as a practical translation of showing up. Surely, simply being physically close with someone in the same room does not automatically guarantee any positive outcomes to bring you closer mentally, unless you are intentional about placing the other person in the front of mind first by making things personalised and convenient, rather than being entitled or merely hopeful. With hybrid working trending in the post-pandemic era, always ask yourself: Where can I trade convenience in for connection? How can I get things done more productively but also preserve the opportunities to meet and deepen my relationship with other people?

With the entire chapter dedicated to the benefits of communicating and overcommunicating, it should have provided more reasons for you to be more vulnerable, tangible and thereby 'connectable'. Author and public speaker John Powell once said, '(c)ommunication works for those who work at it.' Acknowledging this, I would like to add that communication works for those who are driven by the reward and pleasure, rather than fear and pain.

CHAPTER 11

HURDLES ARE NOT BARRIERS

"Where the loser saw barriers, the winner saw hurdles."
— Robert Breault

As your language skills grow with time and experience, you should be able to keep on top of your basics in a foreign environment, where you have already built a base of social network locally. Nonetheless, as far as you have come in a non-native language, does the notion still hit you that you have many contacts but few people to share your highs and lows with? This phenomenon is an epidemic worldwide with individualism on the rise in many societies at an accelerating rate exacerbated by the COVID-19 pandemic. In parallel, social research in the recent decade already shed the light that for almost 50% of the time we overestimate our relationship with the other person and we are extremely prone to do so when we are in need.

If the above study results strike you, reflect on these questions: Do you sometimes comprehend what people say and write in the language but still don't quite understand the other person's thoughts and behaviours? Do you feel that even though people see and listen to you communicating in a foreign language you still don't feel genuinely heard and appreciated? Do you struggle to foster genuine and meaningful connection in addition to the functional and transactional agenda which connected you and the other person together in the first place?

Whatever you set out to do, there will be difficulties and obstacles along the way, both envisaged and unexpected. There is no exception to turning a stranger into a contact, a contact into a connection and so forth. Without discounting this, in light of the opening quote, I want to highlight the distinction between a hurdle and barrier. Both physically and metaphorically, a hurdle by definition is an obstacle you can jump over whereas a barrier is an obstacle that prevents movement or access which usually takes more effort and resources to break and deconstruct rather than being able to just leapfrog over it. It is in this spirit that I created this chapter to help you redefine the hurdles and barriers on your journey to diversify and advance your connections.

ARE YOU WELL PLACED IN YOUR OWN MIND FIRST?

As an enabling step to become more valued and recognized by your network, you are responsible for knowing how you perceive yourself and the person you're speaking to before trying to influence their perceptions of you. In a state of expectancy where

MULTILINGUAL CONNECTORS

we wish other people could support and recognize us or simply become a closer friend, we usually tend to attach high importance over them in our minds, which can then influence our behaviour and even self-esteem. For those having qualms about their abilities to command a foreign language, possibly you, the sense of power imbalance is often intensified. Acknowledging this, you must recognize that even though we can constantly grow our skills in and beyond a language over time, there will inevitably always be someone ahead of us in any arena. This means over the course of our life we will keep a degree of dependence on other people. Whilst it can sometimes be really challenging to see ourselves as equal to some people, we should always attempt to see individuals past their job titles, organisation names or any external labels that lead us in front of them. We should seek to explore their personal characters and common interests other than the key agenda (e.g. hobbies, non-for-profit community projects) which can bridge the distance between you.

Further to the above, you must distinguish that while professional conduct and good demeanour are key baselines, they are not the launch pad to another level of connection. Being polite and professional may keep you in your role and generally respected, but still at arm's length from someone you admire and wish to know more, gain recognition from and grow closer relationships with. In both professional and non-professional settings there is nothing inherently problematic about courtesy and etiquette. Yet bear in mind that one cannot simply be trusted or impressive by being polite and professional in most instances. It also doesn't make connecting easier if you keep coming off too humble and thereby distant, as simply an average colleague or acquaintance.

The results of your actions may often only reinforce your beliefs about your power and status in that relationship that generate the exact corresponding results in real life. For instance, if you only see your director as someone who has positional power over you and can influence your pay rise and promotion, you may behave subserviently whilst desperately scratching your head to gain their respect. How can a busy director easily keep you top of mind for a coveted project if you appear reserved and nervous whenever you meet for work or social events and have no courage to ask questions to explore opportunities or simply invite them to share what is new?

In the same scenario, when you do not get assigned to that job, without further evidence you might easily convince yourself that you have limited competency to influence over the decision or no good standing in the office politics. Such a mentality, if unchanged, will only perpetuate similar experiences in future. Instead, if you set your mind to appreciate an individual on and beyond the professional facade, for their sense of humour, knowledge and mentorship, you may naturally develop and channel the curiosity to learn and integrate these positive traits in a way beneficial to you both. For your own interest, remember, we tend to favour people who are similar to us or appreciate us. On the other hand, you should also make conscious efforts to let the key people of influence learn about you at different levels. You should not zero in on the imbalance in terms of power, status, dedications and returns. As will be further covered at the end of this chapter, you should focus your energy to transform the efforts from one-sided into two-way to where both of you are intentional about keeping each other at the front of the mind.

MULTILINGUAL CONNECTORS

With the role of self-image emphasised multiple times, you can hardly outperform your self-image and must give yourself the respect and recognition you deserve in order to command it from the outside world.

THE DRIVING FORCE

'I've learned that people will forget what you said, people will forget what you did, but people will never forget how you made them feel.' — Maya Angelou

In line with Maya's famous quote, brand strategist, speaker and author Catherine Kaputa contended perception is probably the single most influential driving force in human-to-human connections. Perceptions are generated from the way we choose to present ourselves, consciously or unconsciously, when we interact with others, online and offline, in public and private. It follows that what we have invoked inside the other person sticks around longer than what we have presented outside, to or for these people.

Being nice vs kind vs thoughtful

Though most of us from any cultural background would have grown up being taught to be a good person, we must be cognisant that this can be done and felt to different degrees, which defines the distances between you and others in the network. Most of us are nice most of the time, often to come off as polite and professional. Over time, good manners and friendliness become a standard expectation in many settings.

Whilst the word 'kind' has the same number of letters as 'nice', it is usually hard to be demonstrated in split seconds and tiny actions like a smile and greeting. Kindness requires our willingness to go the extra mile and be more invested in another person with empathy and time. For example, it is nice to text someone with kind words when they have just lost their job or had a break-up. In that case, to extend kindness requires you to spend more time listening and talking to them on the phone or even better, in person with greater companionship when they are in need. As the intention translates into more concrete actions, being kind sets one apart from being superficially easy-going or a general people pleaser. You need to show more respect and attention than normally expected to make people feel cared about.

It is a big step ahead to put concrete actions behind words. You can infinitely improve your grammar, vocabulary, accent and tonality to say beautiful words to others, but if you seldom take well-meaning actions for other people, you are likely to remain being seen as nice or decent but nothing beyond. Worse yet, if you only display your kindness in the words you say, rather than presenting kindness in your actions, you could leave the impression of being all talk and no substance when it comes to the service of others.

There is even another level from going a bit deeper as an empathetic person: being thoughtful. Thoughtfulness goes beyond kindness because it entails nurturing a relationship with someone to understand how and what that person thinks and the other way round. Both qualities of kindness and thoughtfulness have a lot to do with the abovementioned perception as a critical relationship determinant. A kind person leaves the

MULTILINGUAL CONNECTORS

impression of caring more than just being friendly and courteous, as you would with many strangers, acquaintances or colleagues. Someone thoughtful, on top of all the previous, invokes a sense of having a deeper bond within you as that person always tunes into your feelings and translates kind intentions and words into meaningful actions. As we embrace kindness, we should strive to become more thoughtful especially to those with whom we wish to form deeper connections and authentic relationships.

We can pretty much derive being full of thoughts from the formation of the word 'thoughtful'. Exactly as it is at the core, being thoughtful demands greater time and commitment to develop the skills and mentality to pay attention to and tailor actions around an individual's idiosyncrasies. To name a few traits that can uniquely define an individual, it can range from preferences in personal style, food, communication methods, personality, values, short- and long-term goals, to circumstances current or historical either positive or negative (e.g. loss of family members, employment gap, moving to another city, starting a new role). This strengthens the notion that connecting is largely about other people, as adapted from John Maxwell's famous saying.

Note that whilst the differences between kindness and thoughtfulness may seem subtle and nuanced to some, in practice they actually embody two distinct philosophies. A kind person lives by the Golden Rule: Treat others the way you want to be treated. In comparison, a thoughtful person practises the Platinum Rule: Treat others the way they want to be treated. In some religions and cultures, the former is a maxim and can be considered an ethic of reciprocity. A governing conduct, you wish upon yourself what you wish upon others. Whilst the Golden Rule advocates for treating others with humanity and kindness, it has a shaky presumption at its core: that the other person wishes to be treated in the same way as I wish to be treated and vice versa. How can you assume what you deem as favour, dignity and respect is perceived as the same by the other person who may be culturally conditioned differently and live without the exact same values and life philosophy as yours? Therefore, here is the paradox: by fabricating and imposing your self-oriented assumptions upon the other person, you are actually in danger of going against the ideal behind the Golden Rule.

The above may also explain why sometimes the kindness may only be felt by the person sending it but not the person it is targeting and other times, your well-intended actions may even beget counterproductive results making the other person feel offended or embarrassed. It is far from enough to simply care about doing good deeds for other people and do it through your own lens without heeding what others consider to be dignity and respect. In contrast, thoughtfulness is an extrinsic measure since one would not naturally describe himself or herself as a thoughtful person but may use the word when evaluating others. It is a testament to that person who makes you feel understood and cared about, which goes beyond respected.

Here are some examples on how you may practise thoughtfulness in your daily life:

- **On an achievement:**

    Kind: 'Congratulations! Well deserved!' where you sound a lot like the quick suggested, pre-populated responses that you can prompt and send on social apps such as LinkedIn. This hardly

MULTILINGUAL CONNECTORS

sets you apart from many others who send a predictable message as such on this occasion.

Thoughtful: 'Congratulations [name of the person]! Your work is so inspiring on [the project/competition] and valuable [the exact way it did] to [key stakeholders]!' And more personally, add 'Let's celebrate you by [something this person enjoys doing].' A thoughtful person is intentional about reminding other people of their worth, remembers and celebrates this milestone in more personalised means, and references such past wins to reassure them when they face setbacks in future.

- **On a meeting:**

Kind: Logically plan the meeting, extend an invitation for the whole team to join at a convenient time and location and circulate meeting minutes for actions.

Thoughtful: Set up personalised reminders near the event date and inform the participants of parking availability or public transport options to help them plan the trip. Select the venue to suit the occasion and others' personal preferences (e.g. booking a secluded meeting room for greater privacy, catering with a variety of food for the attendees from different cultures, meeting at the team members' favourite cafe). Personalise the messages when sending the meeting minutes to different parties and highlight the key matters and actions for their attention. These extra efforts not only make things convenient for the others, it also makes them feel their participation is valued.

- **On failure and hardship:**

Kind: 'I am so sorry to hear that. I hope you're coping well and things will get better.' Personally, I would be cautious about using 'Don't worry' or 'You'll be fine' in the response, for it is nearly impossible to accurately gauge how the other person has been impacted even if we might share similar experiences.

Thoughtful: You should check up on people going through difficulties and challenges, but only if you have established it is their desire to be checked up on. Firstly, seek to understand if the person wants to talk about a tough topic which can be quite personal. Then if he or she does, one can say, 'I'm so sorry for your loss/struggles. How can I help you through this? If it helps to stay and talk to someone, I am available to call/meet you at [time] and/or [location] if that works for you.' Beware that you may need to do the check-in multiple times depending on the severity of the situation, which requires you to stay in touch and abreast with that person.

To translate speaking or meaning kindness into doing thoughtful things entails intentional planning and organisation which should ultimately lend itself to execution and follow-through. It is totally worthwhile to go the extra mile to understand someone else's values and ideals. This way, you can better serve them the way they want to and as your connection takes deeper roots, this will be reciprocated.

HOW TO LET THEM OPEN UP TO YOU

A critical measure of the depth of your relationship is how much the other person is willing to disclose his/her private and often vulnerable feelings in your presence. It is one of the most powerful human needs to be seen and heard as we all desire to feel that we matter at various times. Psychologists have discovered we need to express ourselves to feel secure and expressing our needs eases our deep survival fears. Since human beings are born with no other survival skills than the ability to express pain, when we withhold the urge to be heard, we feel helpless and endangered.

Truly, self-disclosure is significant in the development of close relationships, whereby a person reveals private feelings, thoughts, beliefs, or attitudes to another person. According to research in the 1990s, those who engage in intimate disclosures tend to be liked more than those who disclose less. People also get to like others more as a result of having confided in them. The lesson being, by leveraging the disclosure-liking effects, we can transform ourselves from a stranger or acquaintance into a more concrete friend and confidant to our valued connections. As self-disclosure is inherently risky, it makes sense that people will be selective when revealing private feelings, thoughts, beliefs, or attitudes to others. If you want to position yourself as a more reliable and trustworthy confidant to your important connections, you must first know how to motivate them to talk to you more closely.

Further to the above, the aforementioned study also revealed that people disclose more to those who they like initially. This underscores the importance of rapport and trust building ability. Equally important is letting the other person's willingness to open up carry on in the succeeding process. If you believe you are limited by your language skills to let people confide in you, especially when you struggle with expressing with the right words, here are four critical steps to help you minimise the impact of language skills:

1. **Stay non-judgmental from the inside out to decrease the risks of self-disclosure to that person:**
The reason for struggling in self-disclosure is multi-pronged. First and foremost, studies show the anticipated risks will also increase with the depth and amount they open up which may invoke some negative and unethical thoughts and painful memories. You must remember how vulnerable that person is when getting something off your chest regarding often tough subjects. We can feel intimate with someone simply because we feel safe and secure when opening ourselves up to him or her. We may not even anticipate that person to provide any concrete response or advice, as long as they get to see the version of us normally unknown to others and allow it to exist.

Avoiding verbally judging others does not guarantee the right attitude that aligns with the behaviour. Humbleness is a key hurdle to non-judgement. As already highlighted in the previous section on thoughtfulness, you should never assume you know a lot about someone's situation and be too confident about your ability to relate 100% to their feelings. Neither should you feel superior to anyone assuming you know better than them, even if you may have overcome the challenges in a similar situation. Without a humble attitude, you may easily jump to conclusions, disagree and criticise them which derails the conversation where you are supposed to be listening to, not debating with that person.

To display non-judgment, you must handle your own emotions well. As human emotions are contagious, your emotional state will be inevitably affected when attempting to listen and resonate with someone on often stressful matters. When you feel

MULTILINGUAL CONNECTORS

too burdened emotionally, you may unconsciously say things to wrap up the talk and push the load off your shoulders. 'Don't overthink too much.' 'Think about the positive more …' Even when we mean well to cheer the other person up, imposing a sense of hope can be counterproductive by making a distressed person feel his or her feelings are not acknowledged or accepted. Whilst we know the power of optimism, we should also be compassionate and considerate to give other people the permission to experience the full spectrum of emotions at challenging times before they pick themselves up and move on. If the listener does not provide a receptive response, the individual can feel subtly denied, criticised or even more hurt after sharing.

2. **Offer a sense of comfort and security:**

In light of the above, you do not need to worry about saying much in words but must consciously maintain the feeling of security in your presence. Even if you do intend to be all ears and offer emotional support, your words and expressions may be misinterpreted by the individual under stress, who can then feel misunderstood, judged or even overlooked, reinforcing the belief that opening up is risky.

At the core of emotional security is to let others feel your approval and reassurance. The person must be assured that his/her feelings in the moment are valid and can be accepted. You can use simple words and phrases expressing agreement and acceptance such as 'Yes. I agree.' 'True.' or just affirming expressions and gestures when listening and sitting with their emotions.

Be mindful not to attempt to downplay or dilute the person's emotion by reassurance. For instance, if he/she is stressing over work, it can be counterproductive to respond with 'I know!

Everyone has something to deal with. Life is hard.' At the words you somehow seem to acknowledge what that person is experiencing but actually fail to, making them feel they are overreacting on the challenges an average human being needs to go through.

At basic levels you should know better than to talk over someone who needs your non-judgemental listening and emotional acceptance. When using your non-native language in such settings, you should not stress about responding immediately and feel awkward about the silence when you may struggle to articulate. Under such a situation, silence actually gives the person talking to you some space to breathe and process the thoughts and emotions in real time so as to continue without feeling pressured or rushed.

3. **Explore his/her thoughts with that person together:**

In the previous two steps, you may already have gained a preliminary understanding of that person's problems. To further understand their real thoughts, you need to do two important things: restatement and asking open-ended questions.

When you restate, you repeat and paraphrase what the person just said in a way that is more concise and to the point. Though this might be challenging for some non-native speakers, it is a valuable skill to improve overtime. Typically, you can begin your restatement with 'I heard you just mentioned … ' 'It sounds like … ' 'From my understanding, you were just saying … ' Note that the other person should always be at the core of your recount. Even if he or she keeps talking about others like their colleagues and families causing some issues, you can't just follow your curiosity to dig down. Rather, you should seek to help the person revert back to the focal point, namely how they are concerned by

MULTILINGUAL CONNECTORS

the issue. This way, you demonstrate you really care about and pay attention to the person in front of you.

Besides the above, open-ended questions also enable you to gather more information to expand your understanding and verify what you have already understood or assumed. Be careful to sound gentle and slow and do not appear you are aggressively interrogating or educating the other. Let the person feel your well-intended curiosity and kindness rather than doubt or scepticism. Do not make the question too long or ask more than one question at a time so that others will be lost which one to start addressing first or miss some of key elements you wish to know.

4. **Encourage the person to reflect on and express their feelings:**

Up to now, he or she may be one step away from revealing their true feelings to you. You should assist the person in pinpointing the exact emotions because normally they may not express the emotion in words but merely be emotional when they speak with you. In helping them recognize the emotions, without formal psychological training, you could simply probe like this: 'You look very upset when your manager did not take your idea on board. Am I right?', 'You just said you were rejected for an interview but you do look very calm now. Are you actually disappointed?' Depending on your level in a foreign language, you may need to spend some time to pick up some common vocabulary for different emotions and use the right ones to be effective.

Furthermore, self-disclosure does not need to be always one way. You may share your own feelings in a similar scenario to help the person recognize and express their emotions. For example:

'I remember feeling super nervous when talking to the new colleagues and worried about making mistakes when I just started in my company. I wonder whether you are also feeling this way now?', 'I would also feel quite nervous under the situation you just said.' Always remember to let the dialogue pivot around the other person and only share your own story with the intent of assisting in the other person's reflection.

From the above, it is clear that there are way more elements than how much and how well you talk in a language that shapes how you make the others feel in your company. Note you can apply the above steps not only in critical situations to be a valuable support to others, but also build productive conversational habits in getting to know others better.

THE PROMISE OF SHOWING UP

As basic as it may sound, you need to be seen as much as possible in front of people's eyes to remain and resurface at the front of their minds. To interpret this notion literally, meeting face-to-face naturally exposes non-native speakers to talking spontaneously which can be intimidating in some settings, but there are enormous benefits of showing up in person with visibility top of the list.

After starting my bachelor's degree in Melbourne, I struggled in managing my workload and barely socialised. Deep down, I felt outcast and unsatisfied. Because of such unpleasant early experiences, I would never forget how showing up paved the way to an expanded realm of opportunities. When I was in my

MULTILINGUAL CONNECTORS

second university year, not only was I active on multiple student committees to organize professional development events, I would also proactively promote them in lectures even without officially assuming the role of marketing. Back then, my Chinese accent was thick and presentation skills far from mature, but I just spoke with deep faith in their value to my peers, in anticipation of a decent turnout. In the same year, I began job seeking in my discipline though I did not feel highly confident or entitled given my qualifications. Neither was I counting on landing a job immediately through the career events I contributed to organising. Eventually, when I emailed a lecturer to be my referee on the CV, he ended up going an extra step beyond my expectation and introduced me to my first boss. He wouldn't otherwise have had a face to my name among many students had he not experienced me in person several times, typically through these marketing presentations which rendered me a proactive candidate and peer leader apart from being academically high-performing.

Though foreign language anxiety kept haunting me down the track, with strong faith in the promise of showing up which I already experienced, I became more active in volunteering and networking. This built up my social confidence and prepared me to speak on international podcasts and industry panels as well as university teaching. When such opportunities came my way, I had made my background transparent to the key decision makers, sometimes with deliberate efforts. Referencing how I landed my first job, in these instances I must have capitalised on my background to strengthen the 'go-getter' image in others' minds.

In penning this paragraph, I have just attended the award presentation for an industry competition I co-founded where the finalists had the opportunity to intern at a sponsoring company. When the HR in that organisation asked us to recommend job candidates from that cohort, I could not possibly advocate for the winning team who exhibited low-energy in the final presentation which accounted for an immaterial percentage in the rubric. More profoundly, they appeared shy and withdrawn from face-to-face networking throughout the competition journey, especially during the presentation night where they pretty much headed off shortly after collecting the awards. From my collective observation about them, sharing the same cultural background, it's not hard to imagine the challenge of speaking English for them. Recalling from my own experience where I benefited from showing up despite imperfect language skills, I only wished they had stayed behind that night to hear me sharing my story and the key criteria for that internship and similar roles they may not be intimately aware of, particularly from a social perspective. I could have also learnt about them better and advised where I could to assist in their career. The final outcome of the intern recruitment was pretty much self-evident.

To varying degrees, turning up and presenting yourself in front of others can be daunting and make you feel extremely vulnerable and self-conscious. I have no intention to downplay the internal battle anyone speaking in a foreign language could be fighting from time to time. Just know, as you choose to take a step back, the whole 'you' fades away from others, not just the parts of you that you don't want others to see. Crucially, for as long as you might be able to hide your weaknesses, you also veil your strengths.

MULTILINGUAL CONNECTORS

BETWEEN LESS BOUNDARIES AND BOUNDARYLESS

"We should see ourselves as a whole and integrated person, not as someone splintered into a million tiny pieces that must be kept isolated." — Rebecca Fraser-Thrill

To put the above idea in practice can seem tricky either online and offline as many people tend to think and keep their personal and professional life in separate compartments. We often see people's online presence differing a lot between professional social media platforms like LinkedIn from the less formal personal ones such as Instagram and Facebook. Overall, on both professional and personal social platforms, there are people who have reservations about oversharing and overexposing themselves and you may be one of them.

My take on this is that there is a fine line between displaying yourself as a textured human being with the perspectives, values, character, personality and lifestyle that make you 'YOU', versus disclosing details too intimate or specific to you to be relevant or relatable for your broader network. Even in the professional realm, a window of opportunity does exist to embellish your professional facade to personalise your professional brand without getting too personal, both online and offline in practice. The inherent promise of showing your multidimensional self is for people to know and connect with you more easily on the commonalities and idiosyncrasies not visible to them before such intentional efforts.

In the online arena, I've reaped the tremendous benefits of

showing more of who I am overcoming fear and perfectionism. Specifically, I was surprised to discover my interest in classical music blurred the personal and professional boundaries of my connections and made the ground for connecting even more boundless.

When I finally afforded my own piano in Australia three years after arrival, I had already grown into the habit of sharing moments in English on social media. The new routine in formation was the marriage of the two activities I highly enjoyed: playing classical music and posting in English about the practice specifically and life recently. Down the track, however, I attracted negative comments from some sophisticated players, including friends. For a while, it hurt my ego and self-esteem as they invoked the memories of my formative years and I could virtually hear the critical voices echoing in my headspace again from parents and tutors. The voices of doubts could not be any louder inside me: Is it really a good idea to post piano videos and subject myself to scrutiny and criticism? Who am I to post since my videos could not be sourced as educational materials like those on YouTube? Should I stop loosely using such expressions as 'I nailed it' in my post when the recording is actually flawed?

I eventually pulled myself back into the base camp mentally and resumed the activities. Regaining perspective, these videos were records of my growth and signified my dedication and perseverance to hone my skills in the margins of hectic university life and work. Regardless of how others perceive my competency, my own progress does give me a sense of accomplishment which boosts my confidence and performance in other realms of life. I also recalled my genuine intention to share the joyful experience

MULTILINGUAL CONNECTORS

with those browsing my feed, amongst whom quite a few commended me and made my day. Other than what I played, many people admired me for simply making time to keep a hobby and posting a glance into my life as someone 'busy busy but killing it all'. In fact, I should take pride in the thought that I was already recognized as a living breathing example of such a lifestyle I had hardly envisaged as possible.

A year from there, an acquaintance invited me to play in a multicultural conference with over 300 attendees in the Arts Centre Melbourne. Before that I did not even think about approaching that friend from the organising committee because I barely believed I would be eligible for performing as someone who simply enjoys playing as a hobby without prestigious awards and qualifications. When I saw her invitation, I almost suspected I was dreaming. 'I have been following you on Facebook. You play so well and my colleagues watched your videos and really liked them. We would love you to play there!'

'Are you sure? I have never performed publicly before and as you know, I am not a professional musician.'

'You do deserve this opportunity! You are clearly very passionate about playing and an inspiration to your peers. Apart from piano, your posts are also amazing! You write so well! I do not often see many international students juggling so many things very well like you! You should definitely show your talent more and share your diverse experience overseas with the attendees as a role model! I'm sure people will enjoy it!'

There, I accomplished my first ever public performance, which sustained the momentum of showing up. Not only was I constantly motivated to post online, I also stepped out to play on public pianos, beginning on campus which I previously would not have dared to. It was a stretch to my mental muscle as it definitely made me even more vulnerable in the public's watch. Yet the reward of showing up was always at the front of my mind to push me out there. While I was not intentional about attracting further performance opportunities, more did come my way. Three years from there, I had played at various public realms in Melbourne, from shopping malls, arts centres and public libraries to town halls and universities. As my hobby became more widely known, it also enriched my relationships as the common language of music became more pronounced with quite a few people I would otherwise only be professionally associated with, such as university lecturers. From there, we exchanged invites to concerts, jazz bars, music festivals, street busking and instrument practice sessions. While enjoying music, we got to know each other better over delightful chats in intimate and relaxing settings which strengthened our bonds.

Whilst the enhanced personal connection through my own initiative did translate into professional outcomes, for me, these are just fringe benefits outweighed by the emotional rewards of the quality social network I was motivated by. Hence, every time I have qualms about engaging in any behaviour that amounts to self promotion and perceive social risks in self-disclosure, I reference past experiences as the above where extended visibility to my other dimensions was well reciprocated and compounded my network in different realms.

Acknowledging all the above, to me, the greatest reward for showing up and confronting the boundaries is not attracting opportunities and accelerating functional outcomes as you

MULTILINGUAL CONNECTORS

become more memorable, credible and likeable. Arguably, we are rewarded the most by ourselves with an elevating and empowering self-image as we break the boundaries over and over.

CHAPTER 12

IT'S OKAY TO DISLIKE NETWORKING

"(T)he end is the means by which you achieve it. Today's step is tomorrow's life. Great ends cannot be attained by base means." — Wilhelm Reich

As far as it's led you to the final chapter, this book is yet to address a reservation that may stop you from due action: what if I have built all the skills and mental resources required but still feel reluctant to put myself out there to network because I don't enjoy doing it?

It may somehow seem like networking is a born gift for some. They often introduce themselves impressively, navigate topics effortlessly and ease in and out of conversations. Even if some people do not use their native language competently or find themselves in an unfamiliar setting, they still exude great confidence and an outgoing personality. They are never left alone

MULTILINGUAL CONNECTORS

in the crowd and often the centre of attention. True, there are people who simply appear to have no qualm about leading conversations or socialising. Compared to those who thrive in social gatherings, networking feels like a big stretch on the edge of some people's comfort zone and even more so for those identifying as non-native speakers, potentially you.

Whether in your native or non-native language, networking could seem like more work than it is worth, whether you're an introvert, extrovert or ambivert. Be it one-on-one or in group settings, with a pressuring sense of 'I need to get something out of it', it feels forced and feels unnatural when you are in the act of what you would typically qualify as networking. Even if social confidence is not a big issue for you, you may still not love networking because you often can't even gain the sheer enjoyment from the interaction let alone any functional outcome expected from it. Despite an abundance of cases where people get a job, sale, business, referral, friend or even partner from networking, you may still see it as superficial, inauthentic and a waste of your time, with any transactional agenda or not.

Therefore, I must address the mindset and philosophy in the above context, in case you doubt you must grow into an active networker or social butterfly to be a Multilingual Connector. Understandably, the prospect of showing up to something you do not really enjoy or view meaningful can be nerve-wracking. What if I tell you Multilingual Connectors don't need to grow more socially oriented than what feels comfortable? What if I tell you one does not have to be well-spoken or talkative to engage well in social interactions? What if I tell you to meet new faces and stay top of mind, you don't have to be physically in front of others as frequently as you can? What if I tell you it is possible to let others get to know you better and remember you well without meeting them often and talking for hours?

In even greater news: building a meaningful social network on your own accord is totally achievable by departing not too far from how you view or approach networking now, so long as you recognize what it is not. Read on for one more piece of the puzzle!

THE MEANS AND ENDS REVISITED

I am not here to do a pep talk to stop you from comparing yourself with the top networkers you know or to glorify networking and motivate you into it. Given where you are in this book, I really hope you recognize that networking is only an act, a process and in essence a means to an end. While a transaction may be an obligation for your personal and business agenda, connection is the core need of human beings. That is, to foster genuine and organic relationships with others which are meaningful in your own eyes that could enrich you mentally, professionally, financially, physically and/or spiritually.

Some social media platforms such as LinkedIn label your contacts as 'connections', creating an illusion of productivity and effectiveness. In the spirit of 'it's who you know not what you know', many people recognise the importance of social networks but often confuse being prolific with being productive in that they generally believe the more people you know the greater the chance to forge meaningful relationships. While this notion appears sound and reasonable, it is important to remember connection is the end goal for any relationship to take root

MULTILINGUAL CONNECTORS

and transactions to happen, as illuminated in the initial chapter. Once you master the art of connecting, the unlocked opportunities are just natural by-products of your ability to establish and maintain meaningful bonds with people.

The desired end results will only manifest when you use the right means for as many times as possible, even with just a small bunch of people you know – a stage one must experience when starting afresh in a new environment. Repeating the act of networking with a higher focus on quantity and breadth, rather than quality and depth, will more than likely give you more contacts than connections. Even if you have advanced to the level where you can easily walk out of a room with a pocketful of business cards, new leads on your mailing list and any kinds of transaction or partnership through successful follow-ups, it may still perpetuate the sense of having many contacts but not as many connections.

From my observation, the Multilingual Connectors who seem truly great at and enjoy networking share a common secret: they aren't actually networking when they appear to be. Rather, they are focusing on the ends more than the means.

A LIFESTYLE, NOT LIVELIHOOD

A mechanical and transactional networking philosophy often makes it more daunting and inauthentic, and will prevent you from ever actually approaching it the right way to forge quality connections. In reality, networking does not feel natural for many people because they tend to see networking as a 'thing', a business or stepping stone. This way, even if the networking leads to concrete functional results, the emotional rewards from connecting are largely lost in the process. I'm in a position to make and reaffirm this statement only because I am fortunate to have experiences that led me to the epiphany fairly early in my life abroad; when you are networking, it feels like a livelihood but when you are connecting, it feels like a lifestyle – one that is truly rewarding and enjoyable.

I was lucky to land my first industry job in Melbourne as a second-year college student and a non-native candidate, in a consulting firm ran by local Australians. The moment I made it through the door, it felt like a huge load off my shoulders – finally, I didn't have to get my head around presenting myself at professional functions, initiating coffee catch-ups, asking for referrals and following up applications to my first job. In my case, I didn't really end up getting my first job that way. Were these past experiences a write-off? Not really in retrospect, because they are incredibly valuable reference points for reflection. I chanced to find myself at a networking drink in my industry after clocking off on the first day. I cannot forget the positive sensations when I told others I had literally just had my first day in our field in super high spirits. Finally! I didn't have to repeat my elevator pitch to highlight where I came from, how much I enjoyed what I was studying and how keen I was for any industry experience to kick-start my career. For the first time in a while, I didn't have to scan the room, take photos of the name tags or attendees at the check-in point and weigh up my time with 'the key people of influence', typically those I would wish to get something career-related from. In the same room, there were some job candidates, some of whom were college students still scrambling to

MULTILINGUAL CONNECTORS

get interviews for a professional role, just like me a few weeks ago. As soon as they learnt about my new job, they were super impressed and wished to know how I found it only in my second year and as an international student who back then was typically disadvantaged by the visa status for even an entry-level job in our field. After picking other people's brains on the same subject for months, I found myself on the other side of the Q&A. My turn! It's my turn to share my experience, from job hunting to the first day at work I'd just had. Openly, I shared my ups and downs in the lead up to being referred by a lecturer to my boss.

'Do you have any tips for me?' In anticipation of this question, the answer came to me as I was sharing my volunteering experience and how enjoyable and rewarding it was, let alone making that lecturer remember me well to make recommendations. 'From my experience, I think we shouldn't do anything only for the sake of getting a job, networking or volunteering, because … uh … because … I think … if you think this way, it kills the fun of these activities.' At that moment, I couldn't have articulated my thoughts at the same clarity and precision as I do now in the English language and I was probably also a bit too excited and a little exhausted on my first working day. I could not see myself as a career expert or seasoned professional to advise but what I ended up saying off the top of my head rings true after a deeper reflection on my experience. True, it kills the fun – doing something in the hope of taking something from someone. It creates performance pressure and blindfolds you on the other benefits of doing what you enjoy that outweighs what you would've expected from the beginning. On that night, for the first time, the notion surfaced in my mind that I really enjoyed organising events to help those colleagues coming from overseas like myself start working in our discipline locally. Though I had counted on volunteering to grow my skills and render my resume to appear more job-ready, I actually expected those senior and more experienced colleagues to benefit from these initiatives sooner than a job came my way. As much as I secretly hoped volunteering could benefit my career, I was dedicated and committed to these roles. To say the least, job aside, I already felt very rewarded by meeting many like-minded and growth-minded colleagues and alumni. I already felt immense joy and reward from sharing my experience and thoughts to support others where I had been, as if I was one of the panel speakers I invited to the career events I assisted in organising.

Following that event, I became more self-initiated to partake in social functions, staying accountable for self-development and diversifying social circles. Without immediate personal agenda at the front of mind and tip of the tongue, I navigated the interactions with greater ease and experienced the same positive feelings over and over again. In the meantime, I compounded my experience in the industry and volunteering ventures, so the opportunities were ample for me to give advice to inspire and guide my peers. As my genuine interest became more and more visible in connecting with people in line with what I was doing, I would organically leave good impressions which translated into introductions and referrals that I'd hardly envisaged initially, such as media features, event collaboration and speaking opportunities. In a nutshell, this was how my social image built up over time as one having a knack for networking in mainstream definitions.

MULTILINGUAL CONNECTORS

From the experiences as the above, it gradually unfolded that it is not exactly the people-facing activities that I gravitate to and find addictive. Being an introvert, I do not largely enjoy pivoting from one person to another in a crowd and would also be selective about small-size meet-ups. With strong faith in the emotional benefits of quality social relationships, it is the seeding and nurturing of strong connections that I integrate into my lifestyle with traditional networking being one of the various means to the ends. I will continue unravelling this perspective in the rest of the book.

FEELING INAUTHENTIC?

We often get such advice as 'be your authentic self' on networking and broadly, social interactions. However, do you usually feel awkward and self-conscious in front of others and therefore find it hard to present your genuine self? From time to time, do you also feel obliged to put additional efforts to display the best sides of yourself to impress? This again exacerbates the feeling that you are 'faking it' and not being truthful which automatically forms the barrier between you and the other person. From experience, speaking in a foreign language can really feel like a mentally straining performance where we exert extra effort and communicate as best as we can. In high-stake settings, such sentiments intensify. When you feel inauthentic, you may likely avoid opportunities to form new relationships, let alone seek them out, according to Marrisa King, author of *Social Chemistry*.

In that book Professor King also argues 'people aren't either authentic or inauthentic.' It is not necessarily morally wrong or dishonest to engage in self-presentation and to adapt to circumstances. In psychology, self-presentation can be construed as the act which involves the processes by which people control how they are perceived by others. Although we cannot fully control the other side of interactions, we can put efforts into considering how the other person may review us and make conscious choices on how we come across and behave when interacting. Even though at first glance this might seem disingenuous, all human beings engage in self-presentation, as part of our everyday decision making at both conscious and subconscious levels, according to Integrative Wellness & Life Coach, Allaya Cooks-Campbell. It is a natural desire to ensure that we show up in a manner that makes us feel positive about ourselves. Even if we may not feel we are confident, competent and likeable all the time, we all want others to see us the way we like to see ourselves as. Stemming from Mark R. Leary's scholarship, strategic or tactical self-presentation is the process which occurs when one seeks to create a desired image or invoke a desired response from others. Given such psychological terms for impression management, it is important to recognize self-presentation and manipulation are distinct. That is, you do not have to feel it is 'dirty' or 'immoral' if you curate your social image and be intentional about making the desirable version of you more visible.

After all, managing how others perceive us can work for their benefit, not just ours. While I get to share the experiences and feelings that render me vulnerable as an immigrant from time to time in both private and public, I am always meticulous about what I convey. Without sugarcoating or downplaying any struggles or hardship I've been through, I make sure optimism and

MULTILINGUAL CONNECTORS

resilience remain the main tone of the stories and lessons – as this not only cements my social image but serves to inspire others. Such efforts are by no means superficial, but essential to show the breadth and depth of your character and experience to educate and inspire others. If you are in the habit of preparing and scripting in advance of social interactions, there is no need to doubt such deliberate effort because it is likely that you do it with the good intention to make the communication smooth, deliver the right message and minimise misunderstanding for your mutual benefits. Whether in your native language or not, preparation for meetings is a manifestation of self-presentation and for the reasons already explained, it should not be seen as self-serving. On this thought, you may recall some occasions where you have the intention to prepare for self-promotion and therefore feel doubtful and hesitant. That's totally fine if you do this with the primary aim of educating others on your strengths and values who may then benefit from them. So far as you recognize or are keen to explore opportunities to provide value, you need to ensure you communicate with the other person's interest at the heart and walk your talk. Again, this is not to be confused with manipulation.

The antidote to the feeling of being inauthentic is not unconditional self-disclosure in the hope that others will appreciate you in your own skin and the gesture of being 'authentic'. A fundamental reason is because other people will not by default care much about what kind of person you are and may still remain distant when you over communicate about yourself. Even if you believe you have exhibited the best version of yourself, you must still ensure there is a reason for the other person to connect with this presentation, be it your appearance, cultural background, social profile, professional experience, personal story, achievements, etc. For other people to care about any of these, there must be something in their interest which they also know you care about. What prevents many people from connecting effectively is the excessive self-focus at the ignorance of other people.

With or without an agenda, on the plan or by sheer coincidence, the experience of connecting will improve tremendously with a greater focus on the others and on giving not just taking. On that first networking evening I joined as a fresh working professional, I actually found myself a changed person among the professionals, many local and high-profiled. Even though I still struggled to finish a glass of beer and was not quite able to consistently keep up with conversations full of industry jargons and 'Aussie' slang, I felt more relaxed and engaged in conversations. With job seeking out of the mind, the focus leaned towards the other person without us talking around the subjects that were very different from those in similar settings previously. As I listened to people relaying their professional journey and came up with questions, I was genuinely following my curiosity instead of asking a question to impress people, demonstrate my maturity, or rather, cover up the opposite. The pressure dissipated to keep the curious mask on towards both the individuals and their organisations where I would wish for a job. Prior to that, I would deliberately search for the information that may be helpful to me and listen for every hook to chime in or usher in another question prepared beforehand to help me 'knock on the door' and convert this into an opportunity. That evening, in a refreshed state of mind, I was more able to tune into the

MULTILINGUAL CONNECTORS

other person's characters and emotions alongside other non-verbal cues that convey something about the individual. Behind all the information and knowledge, there could be a story, a lesson, a wisdom that the other individual couldn't share or share in the same fashion. They can move us, inspire us, enlighten us and sometimes even challenge us as they collide with our own beliefs, values and paradigms. They are the exact fertilisers to make those otherwise superficial, mechanical and agenda-driven interactions humanised and for connections to take root.

Here are the common patterns I've found in some of the most memorable and enjoyable encounters that sparked genuine connections. There's no space for fear of awkward silence as the other person and I are just as content and grateful wherever it ends as where it started. Even in a professional setting, the conversation can veer away from the occupational naturally as curiosity cements about the other person more holistically. This way, it is easy for us to move the attention away from seniority and anything else in our background that may differentiate and distance us. A sense of inclusion made all the participants welcome to share their perspective. As illuminated above, in a typical interaction as such that inspires authentic and organic connections, there is little pressure for excessive self-promotion. I often find myself in the flow speaking in my second language in such conversations, as the mind is primed for both giving and receiving.

Given all the above, I maintain that it is fine to be intentional during networking with some personal agenda. In the increasingly individualistic world today, networking can be problematic and dysfunctional if you don't move away from the single focus on what you want. To humanise the interactions in transactional settings, it is also paramount to note this and that not all relationships need to be founded upon a professional or instrumental agenda. It's indeed a pleasure and privilege to know a person in multiple dimensions, let alone being invited into their emotional world and dreams, even just with a quick glance. We can play to our own agenda, but we also need to make conversations more effortlessly genuine and enjoyable.

BE VALUABLE, NOT JUST SOCIABLE

By definition, a sociable person likes to meet and spend time with other people. In common understanding, it also extends into being willing to talk to others. There is vast research evidence of the health and practical benefits of socialising. Studies have shown being social helps you access social support in a variety of forms: instrumental(practical) support (e.g. give you a lift), emotional support, informational support (advice and guidance) and appraisal. In work settings, socialising can prevent professional burnout. According to a journal article in Oxford University Press, people who have good social connections at work report higher productivity, job satisfaction, leadership effectiveness and higher general well-being. Though the benefits of sociability are widely agreeable, in practice, as stated in the beginning, many people are under the compulsion of becoming more social to live up to societal expectations and accelerate interpersonal success. If this speaks to you and you worry your current level of sociability may disadvantage you, I want to underscore that being a person who is socially oriented does not equal being a person of value.

MULTILINGUAL CONNECTORS

"Try not to become a person of success, but rather try to become a person of value." — Albert Einstein

To explain my point above, here is my understanding of the quote by the great scientist Einstein. Success largely relies on the value you bring to others rather than coming on its own. In other words, your skills, knowledge, experience, credentials and awards do not mean much to others unless you can utilise them to create value. An individual's value can not only be professional or functional, but also emotional whereby others experience positive feelings with you in the company or spirit – which makes the mastery of human psychology and behaviour extremely paramount. Day in and day out, we have numerous social interactions online, in person or both. As time goes by, who will you more likely remember and feel motivated to stay connected with and provide the various types of social support abovementioned? Your perceived value of different people is a key driver.

Up to this point, you may already recall someone you see as a valuable connection who is likeable, supportive and inspirational but does not identify as an extrovert or social butterfly. A person of this kind may not necessarily be someone you frequently interact with. If you still have qualms about the likelihood of missing out on quality connections without networking a lot in the traditional sense, I prompt you to ruminate on Anthony Robbin's famous quote, 'proximity is power'. At first sight, this may intensify your worry that if you do not have a lot of social activities, you will lose proximity with others who can bring positive changes to your life. That said, I hope you recognize the power of proximity is largely conditional according to his original saying:

> *"Proximity is power. If you can get proximity with people that are the best in the world, things can happen because all of the people they know, the insights they have and the life experience they have. They can save you a decade of time by one insight."*

It follows that it does not suffice to socialise as frequently and extensively as you can with as many new people as possible. Rather, the focal point should be connecting with the 'right people' as illuminated in Chapter 9, and even more so, being someone who will attract quality connections on your way. As the quote indicates, one has the power to change others' lives for good if he or she possesses the knowledge, insight and life experience. In my own understanding, to change other people's lives and in turn that of our own for good also requires the heart set and mindset of servitude. When what you can offer becomes tangible which matches the needs and wants of those who cross your path, you can identify as an individual of tremendous value at the front of other's minds.

Recalling how an individual value can be defined in the broad spectrum of criteria, here are the important habits I recommend you cultivate and maintain to be a valuable person in the eyes of others and yourself:

1. **Be committed to self-development:**

Strive to become more resourceful and myriad-minded. You don't need to know or be an expert at everything but you should pinpoint the skills you possess and those you need to keep

MULTILINGUAL CONNECTORS

developing and bridging. Further to this, you should package your knowledge and skills as one or multiple points of value to other people, which ideally also aligns with your personal interests and strengths. In addition to being skillful in specific fields, I also champion having versatile knowledge and diverse experience that expand your ability to connect with others on common grounds. Besides, people naturally respect and gravitate to those they see possessing a wide range of knowledge and experience, which simply adds weight to your words and elevates your social image. In the same context, you also become more interesting and memorable because of your knowledge, experience and perspective. I understand for some of you this may not be achievable in a short period of time, but it should surely be the direction you endeavour towards day by day. Equally if not more important than your skill set, mindset as discussed from several angles in this book, is crucial for achieving goals in acquiring and applying the skills.

2. **Contribute to the community:**

You do not really need a job title or position to perform the function of service. Whilst you may need certain skills, resources and qualifications to perform specific tasks, offer advice and provide support, it is more of essence having a heart set oriented towards giving instead of taking and receiving value. As a collective term, a community does not have to be a large group or an organisation. It can simply include those you meet day-to-day, from families, friends, co-workers, acquaintances or even strangers, online and off-line. Be it a major personal or work project or small act of kindness in the routine daily moments, an attitude of servitude can totally affect your perceived worthiness in others' minds and that of your own.

3. **Keep your promises:**

All words no action is no good. Someone who constantly talks about doing something but never takes action or follows through will overtime lose respect and trust from others. Would you believe in the value of someone you see as unreliable and untrustworthy? A large part of being of service is living up to the promises you make to yourself and those promises you make to others. While this may sound like a hygiene factor, keeping one's words is a common notion but less of a common practice. To draw an example in networking scenarios, from time to time you will meet people who leave farewell notes like 'I will DM you XXX's contact and the information on XXX' or 'I'm up for a coffee chat next week' but they don't really respond in the time frame promised. In work settings, there are also plenty cases of commitments to deadlines being poorly communicated in absolute terms which lead to disappointment and eat away at trust. It follows that what's simple to do is also simple not to do. Even a small contact exchange or follow-up message in promise can weigh much more in the minds of the receiver being expectant than you would've anticipated. Walking your talk not only earns you trust, it is also conducive to your self-image and confidence, because other people will only have faith in you if you have faith in yourself, by consistently keeping your promises!

4. **Advance communication skills:**

Whether you identify as a non-native speaker or not in any setting, you are not exempt from this to let your message be heard effectively so that others know what type of person you are and what you are capable of. This book shines light on various important communication elements aside from the technicality of language to help you navigate communication challenges with those from a different culture. A vital quality of a Multilingual Connector who not only communicates but connects well is the sensitivity towards others' needs and wants by creating an avenue for open and effective communication.

5. **Positive attitude:**

What you have to offer does not always need to be tangible or functional. A positive attitude is one of the greatest values you can provide to yourself and others. Not only does a positive attitude allow you to be better performing on the value-adding tasks, it also is contagious. People love to be around those who have an optimistic outlook and learn to see the good in every situation and the opposite also holds true. You will be perceived as a valuable asset if you can spread positive energy to those you engage with. To be scripted in positivity, you need to embrace an attitude of gratitude. Your mind is like a torch, give it a focus to make it content and thankful for whatever comes your way.

6. **Value your time:**

If you wish to be regarded as a person of value by yourself and others, then you need to upgrade how you spend your time and add more value to your life. Other people are unlikely to value your time if you do not value your own time in the first place and they sense this. I used to worry about letting people down and losing them by often rejecting the invitations in conflict with my key commitments including self development and mentoring which occupies me more and more over time. I would really love to hang out with them but I am cognizant I must be accountable for establishing myself in Australia to be an asset in the organisation and community. In the grand scheme of my goals and vision, I do have these people I wish to give back to one day. When you demonstrate you invest your time wisely and intentionally by committing to personal growth and serving others, you will eventually become and in turn appear more resourceful in the eyes of others as the realm of opportunities expands for you to create value with your expanding knowledge and skills. It is true that some people may not savour the gesture of you setting boundaries for your time and may even feel hurt or distanced at first. However, as people see your behaviours paying dividends in tangible outcomes, some of them should respect and appreciate you and new opportunities may emerge for you to connect which would not have existed earlier. Also, as you continue expanding, I guarantee valuable connections and champions will keep compounding in your circle.

As a concluding note at the tail end of the book: do not just be obsessed with networking and connecting. Be obsessed with creating value, as a lifestyle, not just livelihood.

ABOUT THE AUTHOR

Daisy's purpose is to disrupt the common narratives to enable non-native (English) speakers to build meaningful connections across cultures – not through language mastery but self-mastery, a glaring gap in mainstream language and communication training.

She has strong faith in the unique advantages of non-native speakers to unlock opportunities on a foreign land without advanced language levels. Realising conventional education and societal customs are trapping millions of promising non-native speakers in mental prisons and unproductive pivots around language acquisition, she is committed to re-educating people like her to maximise their unparalleled edge via powerful mental frameworks.

Daisy was once isolated, pigeonholed and even barely finding anyone to practice English with after moving to Melbourne in 2015. She got excellent university grades but hardly made connections who would support her at her low points or kept her top of mind to make introductions. She felt nervous and awkward around English-speaking people. Her experience created the illusion that things would get better only if her English was better.

Over time, she spoke better English but still had few connections among many contacts, which cost her countless opportunities and kept her struggling interpersonally. She realized she must work on something other than the language.

As she discovered the missing pieces of the puzzle, she did the exact opposite of fixing her English to appear more 'native-like' or extroverted to 'fit in'. She retained and sharpened her immigrant's and introvert's edge which carved out her achievement-oriented trajectory with a diverse multicultural network.

To transform the status quo for people who share the pains like her years ago, she founded Multilingual Connectors to fill the gap in mentoring to provide the antidote to language mastery for those with a burning desire to stop being unseen, unheard and unappreciated in foreign environment and build their tribes to lead a fulfilling life.

Website: www.multilingualconnectors.com
LinkedIn: Daisy Wu

www.ingramcontent.com/pod-product-compliance
Lightning Source LLC
Chambersburg PA
CBHW022045290426
44109CB00014B/992